# AARON COPLAND

*His Life and Times*

# AARON

# COPLAND

*His Life and Times*

BY ARNOLD DOBRIN

*Thomas Y. Crowell Company    New York*

Acknowledgment is made to the following publishers for permission to quote from copyrighted material:

From *Dance to the Piper,* copyright © 1962, by Agnes De Mille. Reprinted by permission of Atlantic–Little, Brown and Company, Publishers.

From *Music, My Way of Life* by Aaron Copland. Copyright © by Aaron Copland. Reprinted by permission of *Boys' Life* Magazine.

From *Copland on Music* by Aaron Copland. Copyright © 1944, 1945, 1948, 1949, 1951, 1953, 1956, 1960 by Aaron Copland. Reprinted by permission of Doubleday & Company, Inc.

From *The American Cause* by Archibald MacLeish. Copyright © 1941 by Archibald MacLeish. Reprinted by permission of Duell, Sloane & Pearce, Meredith Press.

From *Music and Imagination* by Aaron Copland. Copyright © 1952 by Harvard University Press. Reprinted by permission of Harvard University Press.

From *Our New Music* by Aaron Copland. Copyright © 1944, 1945, 1948, 1949, 1951, 1953, 1955, 1956, 1960 by McGraw-Hill Book Co. Reprinted by permission of the McGraw-Hill Book Co.

Designed by SALLIE BALDWIN

Manufactured in the United States of America
L.C. Card 67–15398
2 3 4 5 6 7 8 9 10

*For his cooperation and generosity, the precious time given so freely to our many interviews, his invaluable help and guidance in the preparation of the manuscript as well as its final reading—I am deeply grateful to Aaron Copland.*

# ACKNOWLEDGMENTS

The author wishes to make grateful acknowledgment to the librarians of the Westport Public Library, Westport, Conn., and to the librarians of the New York Public Library at Lincoln Center; to David Walker, Ruth Steinkraus-Cohen, Leonard Bernstein, Erik Johns, and Martha Graham.

*For My Parents*

# Contents

# Contents

# AARON COPLAND
*His Life and Times*

# I

## *America, America*

It was Monday—or perhaps it was Tuesday or Wednesday. Aaron wasn't sure anymore. Not since that day last week when he had abruptly been sent home from school with a rasping throat and a bad case of chills. Since then, everything had been turned upside down. There were no classes or regular meals, no studies or playing. All that time he had been in bed, sleeping or tossing feverishly about. Occasionally he was aware of whispered conversations at the door of his bedroom, and off and on throughout the day he would feel his mother's cool hand rest lightly on his burning forehead. He heard the words "typhoid fever," and not long after, "a light case." Before long the fever began to subside and he started to be more aware of the world around him, began to listen to the noises of the street that came in through the open win-

1

dow. Washington Avenue was a busy street in Brooklyn, New York, and most of the day it was thronged with shoppers. Above the sound of their voices Aaron could hear the calls of the vendors describing the advantages of their vegetables and fruit, and suddenly he realized the fresh fruit was what he had been craving—for it was just the beginning of summer.

Before long his appetite had been sated by a plate of new peaches and apricots, and especially by some delicious cherries, his favorite fruit. It had been the gift of his brother's wife, a thoughtful gift that required an equally thoughtful acknowledgment of thanks.

Aaron Copland—eight years old but already aware of the pleasure of creativity—scrambled out of bed to get a pencil and paper. Within an hour he had written a poem of thanks to the kind woman with such a good memory. It was the first creative work he had attempted.

The classes in English and music were always Aaron's favorites. But the school courses were not to open up the world of music for him; that was a way he would have to find for himself. It was to be a while before he would begin the search in earnest, but in the meantime there was much to see and learn.

That year the winter came early. The weather was sharp and crisp and there was a festive air about as the Copland family busily prepared for the annual visit of their relatives from the South who came to work in the Copland department store at Christmas time.

There was an atmosphere of high expectation and fun

as the holidays approached and yet, for a young Jewish child, these happy times brought a certain sense of questioning and bewilderment. The public schools closed for the two week Christmas vacation, gifts were exchanged, and Santa Claus was eagerly discussed. In all these preparations the Jewish children were involved while, at the same time, they were not involved.

The unfamiliar religious traditions were confusing, as was the disturbing question of allegiance. For Hanukkah, the Jewish Festival of Lights, came at almost the same time. It was all very puzzling, but still there was much fun to be had. And when all the relatives gathered together at mealtimes, there were interesting stories to listen to, gossip about births and marriages, and talk of the past—a past utterly unlike the life they now knew.

Some of Aaron's aunts and uncles spoke with a foreign accent, as did his father, Harris Copland. They had come from eastern Europe not too many years ago and the lives they had lived there were still vivid and real for them. Conversation often turned to the "old country." It had been a hard life, one which became increasingly severe and painful as the nineteenth century came to a close.

For over a thousand years the population of Europe had remained relatively constant. But in the late eighteenth century, as men discovered new ways to produce more food and new laws of hygiene, the population rapidly began to grow. Factories were built and new machinery introduced. Peasants reacted with fear, alarm, and sometimes violence as they saw the familiar patterns of life disrupted. In several countries, particularly in

Russia, the nobility went to extreme lengths to focus the peasants' attention on something else. They did not have to look far, for the Jewish people had always been a convenient scapegoat when a victim was needed.

In Russia severe laws were passed that forced the Jewish people into a life of greater deprivation and misery than they had known for decades. Long herded into a settlement on the western border of Russia, they were now forced from the smaller villages into towns where the overcrowded conditions and desperate poverty made life unbearable. When new efforts were made to enforce military conscription into an army that was known for its brutality and corruption, nothing was left but to escape.

The young men, who were generally the first to go, quickly sent letters home telling of the opportunities that awaited all immigrants to the New World. Before long they were sending money too, for these young people felt a deep sense of obligation to those who had been left behind. As soon as they were able, wives, brothers, and sisters followed. Generally the last to leave were the old people. The migration west quickly became well organized as a constant flow of immigrants streamed into the port cities of Danzig, Bremen, Odessa, and Naples.

Perhaps in their letters home the imaginations of these new immigrants became overly inflamed, for the legend of the fabulous riches of America grew stronger. Many little children who had come on the long journey with their parents through the forests and towns of central Europe, half asleep in wagons, carts, and trains, listened with unbelieving ears as their parents discussed the new country that awaited them. No fairy tale or legend of the distant past could conjure up such wondrous images as the stories they told. America! Where one had enough food to eat, clean clothes all the time, freedom to travel and to worship as they wished, and yes—where even the streets were paved with gold!

After their crossing of the rough North Atlantic, often a trip that lasted as long as twenty days, many of the immigrants arrived pale and exhausted. Most of the time was spent in the steerage, a section of the ship that derived its name from the hold which was originally intended for animals. But the heat and odors were often as unbearable as the gales that swept across the open decks above. These, together with the rolling and heaving of the ship, left an indelible memory of misery that many were to carry with them all their lives.

Before long the immigrants were pouring into the cities of the eastern seaboard. They found that the streets were not paved with gold; in fact, most of them were not paved at all. Working conditions were often worse than those they had left at home. It was not easy to work eighteen hours daily in a sweatshop and still find the energy for school in the evening—but many did. And late at night, in the walk-ups, the cold-water flats, and jam-packed tenements, they studied the strange new language they would need for the skills and knowledge that led to a better life. In America, every man was on his own.

If the immigrant couldn't afford to buy a shop and didn't want a regular job, he could always peddle from a cart. In Brooklyn, as on the Lower East Side of Man-

hattan, the pushcarts filled the streets and contributed to
the boisterous, swelling current of life that flowed around
them. Almost anything could be bought from these carts
—all kinds of bric-a-brac, kitchen utensils, old books,
yard goods, shoes, and food.

Older immigrants who were prosperous enough to own
their own shop lived lives that rarely moved beyond the
confines of their businesses, napping on a couch that was
hidden behind a curtain in the back and stopping off and
on throughout the day for a glass of tea, Russian style,
with their wives or a few cronies.

Everywhere the immigrants settled in groups that had
a similar background, for they were drawn to others who
had the same habits and spoke the same language. Their
distrust of foreign ways and beliefs continued, but already the dissolution of the old rigid patterns had begun.
For in America one did not have to cross frontiers and go
hundreds of miles to see the strange ways of the foreigner
—he had only to go across the street.

So the various cultures touched and overlapped. Gro-
cery stores might specialize in Italian or Jewish foods but
in the street all the delicious aromas of the salamis,
cheeses, smoked salmon, and fresh rye bread combined
into one. The restaurants too with their rich goulashes,
spaghetti, and borscht helped to break the old barriers as
people ate the strange new foods and found that in spite
of being foreign, they were really very good.

In the bustling activity of these streets the children
played, tossed balls, rolled hoops, darted in and out
among the pushcarts and wagons. Amid their shouts

and laughter one could hear the bells of the horses' har-
nesses, the  cries of the fishmongers claiming their fish
was so fresh that "it melts like butter in your mouth."
From the windows the women called and chatted to one
another and in the evening, in the summer, whole families gathered on their stoops hoping for a breath of fresh
air from the sea.

In the late eighteen-seventies, when he was not quite
twenty, Harris Copland had come to Brooklyn as a poor
immigrant from Lithuanian Russia. His resourcefulness
and ambition soon gained him a thriving partnership with
his cousin in a small department store and enough confidence in his future to think of marriage. Before long
he met Sarah Mittenthal, a girl born in Lithuania but
brought up in the American Middle West. They were
married in 1885 and two years later, feeling more confident and optimistic, Harris severed his partnership with
his cousin and began a business of his own.

Harris Copland brought as much determination and
single-minded interest to bear on his business as Aaron
was later to give to his music. Before his life was over,
he had built a business that was called the "Macy's of
Brooklyn."

But strong and forceful as he was, there was one person whose advice he listened to attentively and often followed. Sarah Copland, although she was a devoted wife
and mother, was the kind of woman who could not find
fulfillment in the routine tasks of housekeeping. Probably
if she had been born fifty years later, and had the benefits

of a higher education, she would have carved out a successful career for herself in one of the professions. But as with so many other women of her time, this vast creative energy was directed to the family business where she spent most of her waking hours. She kept the accounts in the early years, did much of the buying, and was responsible for the displays.

Working together as they did every day in a business that prospered rapidly, keeping a house that functioned smoothly, the Coplands gave their children a deep sense of order and proportion that was to prove a firm foundation for their future lives. It is a tribute to the balance of their values, and their practice of them, that none of the children felt the need of rebellion.

Ralph had been the first to arrive, and then, at two-year intervals, Leon, Laurine, and Josephine were born. Harris and Sarah now had two boys and two girls and they believed their family to be complete. Seven years passed and the Coplands became an established family with a prosperous business. They had put down strong roots in their adopted country and they planned a happy future for themselves and their children. It was in an atmosphere of gratitude and optimism that they welcomed the new century. In its first year, Aaron, their last child, was born.

# 2

# *The Marvelous Discovery*

Ralph, Leon, Josephine, and Laurine were now leading mysterious grown-up lives of their own. They seemed to come and go the same way that adults did. They talked about people and events outside the Copland home in a way that Aaron often could not comprehend. And yet he never felt a sense of rejection, a feeling of being left out. The imaginative world of music that he was being drawn to was never an escape from an alien reality; neither was it the refuge of a lonely child.

Still, it is unlikely that his older brothers and sisters had much time left for their little brother who was still playing with toys while they were already enjoying teen-age activities. Ralph, whom Aaron always thought of as the most intellectual of the family, later became a lawyer. Leon and Josephine had practical minds and were often occupied in the store. They gave Aaron less attention than Laurine, who was fond of music and looked forward to the time when she could join the Metropolitan Choral School. Afterschool hours had to be divided between study, work in the family store, and sometimes amusement. The Coplands were a busy, conscientious family, and duties—of which there were a good many for each member—were expected to be fulfilled promptly and efficiently.

Usually Aaron's father was down in the store, which occupied the first floor of the Copland building, long before Aaron had his breakfast, and it was not unusual for his mother also to be attending to her duties while he ate his first meal of the day. It was the patient Lils, a Negro woman from Barbados, who cooked and cleaned and served Aaron most of his meals. Aaron was devoted to the warm, gentle woman who, as things turned out, had a gift of prophecy. In the days before swing had any musical connotation she often would say to the young precocious boy, "Some day you're going to be swingin' in circles!" meaning, of course, that someday he was going to be *somebody*.

Unusual musical talent is most often found among those who have been born into families with a strong musical tradition. With a few exceptions, great musical artists have received their first instructions from their mothers and fathers, often as young as at the age of three. In the field of music—and this includes both composers and interpretative performing artists—the child prodigy is almost a garden variety creature. There is a story of the meeting between the pianist Artur Rubinstein and

Bronislaw Hubermann, the violinist. "You have talent, my child," Hubermann told the younger player. "Work hard and you will go far." Hubermann was then nine, Rubinstein four.

Aaron Copland was to be eleven before the full, conscious realization came: "I like music—very much. I want to study music. I want to *be* a musician."

In the meantime, the world of early childhood flowed on around him. Outside, the sidewalks, streets, and apartment house stoops were the children's only playground, a spawning ground, as later years proved, of some of New York's greatest talent. It was here that the neighborhood gangs were formed, their quarrels begun and settled, and where their rough games took place. The nationality or religion of a boy's parents determined the group he belonged to and its barriers were as impassable as some of the frontiers from which their parents had actually fled. Italians formed one group, Germans another, Jews and Irish still others.

Aaron moved away from any kind of involvement with these groups. The world outside his home, with its fiercely competitive sports and passionate fraternal loyalties, was rough and ugly. Aaron drew farther and farther away from it. Outside, it seemed that disorder reigned. But inside his home, in his parents' lives and the life he was making for himself, the reverse seemed to be true. There he saw a definite pattern and a sense of order. Later on, in even his first compositions, Aaron felt a strong impulse to bring every piece he worked on to full realization.

At eleven, Aaron would drop whatever he was doing as soon as he heard the sounds of the piano coming from the front parlor. Nothing that he was doing, no story of adventure or exploration, could hold him once those marvelous sounds of the piano chords struck his ears.

Laurine was practicing.

At first, respecting her need for privacy, Aaron would linger in the hall, listening to the sound of the music as she practiced the scales. But soon that wasn't enough, not nearly enough. He wanted to see how her hands moved, what the black keys meant, why the white keys were white, and what she did with those strange little pedals at the bottom of the piano. And then there was the greatest mystery of all—the amazing way that she deciphered those strange black notes which were scattered all over the pages propped up in front of her.

In the beginning Laurine was annoyed by the intrusion. Then she softened and agreed to show the little boy the most elementary position of the hands. Soon she was aware that her brother's interest was not just a child's ordinary need for diversion or common curiosity. There was a kind of compulsion in the way that he went about learning and the concentration that he brought to bear upon his study. Within six months Laurine was aware that he knew more than she did. With admirable modesty she admitted: "You know more now than I learned in eight years of study. I can't teach you anything else."

For a year and a half Aaron worked alone, reading and studying whatever music came his way. Anything, whether it was a Mozart concerto or the latest ragtime was a new musical experience to savor.

Every day Aaron practiced at the piano. Every day his curiosity mounted as he found his fingers gaining more and more dexterity. He could feel his progress. He knew he was moving ahead, but was convinced that it was not fast enough. The time had come to have a professional teacher.

"I want to study the piano," Aaron said to his mother. Mrs. Copland turned from her work to look at him and frowned slightly. "Laurine is a good teacher for you, Aaron."

"No, Mama, I need a better teacher—a *real* teacher."

"Teachers cost money, Aaron."

But what did money matter when music was the most important thing in the world? "Yes, I know, Mama— but I really want to study music. I want to learn more about it."

Aaron's mother remained unmoved. "No, Aaron, *no.* Not right now. We have spent too much already on the others for music lessons that came to nothing." But Aaron begged again and again, and finally Laurine spoke up for him.

At last Mrs. Copland agreed, but with reluctance. "All right Aaron. If you want to find the teacher yourself, we don't have any objections to your studying."

Well, then—he would find his own way! He asked friends in the neighborhood about their teachers and noticed that one name was mentioned more frequently than any of the others. This was Leopold Wolfsohn, the man whose most brilliant pupils were allowed to play recitals in the Wanamaker Auditorium in Manhattan. Perhaps that image of himself actually playing in the Wanamaker Auditorium hastened Aaron's steps to Leopold Wolf-sohn's studio. He made his decision quickly and was accepted as a student. Before long the weekly session with Wolfsohn was the high point of the week and the dream of playing in the auditorium faded in importance. But it was to become a reality sooner than he thought.

# 3

# *The World Beyond Brooklyn*

When Aaron was twelve he was expected to help in the store. There was always plenty of work to be done—stock that had to be unpacked, marked, or dusted, and errands to be run. In later years he would take charge of the cash register when the cashier was at lunch or on a rest period.

Aaron was paid for his work, but it was assumed that he would be sensible enough to save a part of his earnings, no matter how small they might be at the beginning. The virtues of thrift, hard work, and an orderly life that he had heard so much about and seen practiced in the daily life around him were now to become an even more important part of his own life. Already a sense of balance and proportion in human affairs had become a deep part of his consciousness. The Copland household was a place where fun and pleasure were permitted and

15

encouraged, but only in their place. And that place was the reward for hard work and conscientious fulfillment of responsibility.

To Aaron, the exciting and most important thing was that he now had more money for music and books. His training had cautioned him to spend money judiciously—but spend he did—on new books, new scores, and tickets for concerts.

It was at the Brooklyn Academy of Music, of which Walt Whitman had been so proud fifty years before, that he first heard the great Beethoven, Brahms, and Tchaikovsky symphonies as interpreted by Walter Damrosch, the conductor of the New York Symphony Orchestra.

One concert that Aaron had been looking forward to with great expectation was a performance by the great Polish pianist Ignace Paderewski, who was then at the height of his fame. Aaron wanted to share the experience with someone. His father was out of the question because he never attended concerts. Probably his mother would be too tired. Ralph and Leon were no longer at home and Laurine and Josephine were going to visit friends. Well, so be it. He had found his way by himself before.

Alone that night, listening to and watching Paderewski, who was a composer as well as performer, a new idea began to stir Aaron's imagination. Up to now his future had not been clear to him—simply vague years ahead that were in some way connected with music. For the first time now he realized he wanted to *write* music.

Later on other concerts and dance recitals were to stimulate his interest in the world of music and the theater. Isadora Duncan was one of the great dancing stars of the day. Sergei Diaghilev's Ballet Russe, particularly the oriental splendors of *Scheherazade* and the haunting *L'Après-midi d'un Faune,* to the music of Debussy, were unforgettable experiences.

In those days without television or radio, attending a concert was always a cherished experience, arranged for weeks in advance and remembered with intense pleasure for months and years afterward.

Now, at fifteen, Aaron was beginning to try his hand with compositions of his own, tentatively at first but with rapidly growing confidence. For a composer it was a late development. Many years afterward Copland wrote in *Music and Imagination:*

> My discovery of music was rather like coming upon an unsuspected city—like discovering Paris or Rome if you never before heard of their existence. The excitement of the discovery was enhanced because I came upon a few streets at a time, but before long I began to suspect the full extent of this city.

It accelerated more quickly when he began to frequent the old Brooklyn Public Library on Montague Street which held "riches of which my immediate neighbors were completely unaware." Inside, among the dusty shelves, Aaron experienced an exciting feeling of adventure and exploration as he spent long hours browsing through the books and music scores that were to open new, undreamed-of worlds to him.

Coming home in the evening through the drab, cold

streets with his books and scores tucked safely in a bag, Aaron felt a sense of eager anticipation as he thought of the hours ahead. Home alone in the parlor, he would soon he deeply engrossed in a book or accompanying himself on the piano as he sang the songs of Franz Schubert or Robert Schumann.

Almost every week now he made the discovery of an unfamiliar composer's work. The letters that he wrote at this time are full of the bursting enthusiasm of youth suddenly becoming aware of the great range of human expression. To John Kober, a younger school acquaintance, he wrote: "Could you get the Tschaikovsky 'Pathétique' Symphony No. 6? I heard the Philharmonic play it and I am sure I can show you some beauties in it we missed. It is perfectly ravishing."

Again to John Kober: "I could not resist the temptation of buying that volume of Debussy's songs. I also bought the second volume of Moussorgsky's songs and some Preludes by Scriabin which are very fine."

But many other scores were almost impossible to obtain. Much of the work by composers who were now of special interest to Aaron, men such as Alexander Scriabin, Claude Debussy, and Maurice Ravel, were published only in foreign editions, and when available on the American market, the prices they brought were completely out of reach.

However, he had now found a new source of musical creativity. Gropingly, tentatively, every week saw him giving more and more time to compositions of his own. Time away from the piano or the concert hall was time that was not being lived as fully as he knew it could be.

Already he sensed the pull of creative work that was so compelling that he could conceive of no other life for himself but that dedicated to music. When it is this way with a young artist, then the decision about his future is made and nothing more need be said. It seems to hinge on the degree of passion he feels. When Aaron saw students in later years in whom that passion was lacking, he knew that there was no point in expressing encouragement.

Aaron Copland was now seventeen. He was eager to begin the study of composition, but he was still very naïve about the development of the creative artist. He believed that one could study composition through a correspondence course in much the same way that one learns accounting or business administration.

Soon he realized his mistake. With some embarrassment he asked Leopold Wolfsohn for the name of a reliable teacher. Wolfsohn suggested that Aaron apply to Rubin Goldmark, one of the leading teachers of composition in Manhattan. He was a nephew of Karl Goldmark, the composer of the opera *The Queen of Sheba,* and he had studied with several prominent men in the world of music, including Anton Dvořák. Rubin Goldmark was an important figure in the music world of New York and was a famous toastmaster at musical events. He gave lectures on Wagner and, as Aaron soon realized to his disappointment, was a strict traditionalist who gave no encouragement to modern music.

Aaron studied with Goldmark from 1917 to 1921.

During this period he also continued studying the piano, first with Victor Wittgenstein and then with Clarence Adler. They were years that gave him the essential understanding of fundamentals but he could never quite overcome the feeling of restraint, the yearning to be in touch with more imaginative minds. And gradually the idea came to him that if he really wanted to see and hear many of the exciting new developments in the world of art, he would have to go to Paris. In 1921 it was common for young American artists to yearn to go there and many of them eventually did. Now Aaron found himself becoming fascinated with everything French. Each new concert of music by Ravel or Debussy kindled his imagination, making him more impatient for the time when he could leave Goldmark and New York and somehow find a way to continue his studies in Paris.

# 4

# Departure

Rubin Goldmark, who was trained in the German musical tradition, saw little reason for Aaron Copland's fascination with French art and music. He finally persuaded him to wait one year before going to Paris, but for Aaron it was a year of impatience, frustration, and marking time.

Then, just as Aaron was beginning to make concrete plans to leave for Europe, he saw an advertisement that caught his eye in *Musical America* magazine. It announced the establishment of a School of Music for Americans at Fontainebleau near Paris. The school had been founded by an American organizing committee—headed by Walter Damrosch, the conductor of the New York Symphony Orchestra—who were hoping to make

French musical traditions more easily available for young Americans. Aaron immediately applied for a scholarship and spent the next three weeks in a state of uncomfortable anxiety. Never had he looked forward to the arrival of the postman with such eagerness. Then, one day when he was beginning to lose hope, the official-looking envelope arrived. Aaron's name was among the nine listed as winners of scholarships.

The crucial time had come when he must break with the family tradition, when he must tell his parents that he had absolutely no intention of going into the world of business. It is often one of the first tests an artist must face, and the success with which he severs these ties can be an important factor in his later achievements or failures.

Now, after having watched his parents work so hard every day of their lives, after having heard the old sad stories about his grandparents' struggles in Russia, after knowing that every security and comfort that he possessed had been hard-won—after knowing all this he had to say to them: "I do not want to be a businessman. I want to be a composer."

This was a shocking admission for any father to hear his young son make in 1918. Such people, musicians, artists, and theater people, lived a life totally apart from anything Harris Copland had known. He believed a man was supposed to protect himself as best he could from life's dangers, not expose himself to them even more openly. How could a musician ever know real security? How could he ever hope to support a family?

But even more incredible, Harris now heard that his youngest son wanted to leave the United States, this beloved United States where for the first time in two thousand years the Jewish people had found a home in which they were treated as equal human beings with a right to live and worship as they pleased.

For a man of Harris Copland's time, this was hard to accept. Memories of the insults and humiliations that he had suffered on his way to the New World were still too fresh in his mind. For his young son to want to get an education in a foreign country was not only hard for Harris to understand, it was unthinkable. After all, why should any young Jew want to return to a Europe which, for the men of Harris' generation, was a place of fear, hunger, and religious persecution?

So the conversations that went on between Aaron and his parents, or privately between his parents, or between his parents and their relations, did not revolve only on the relative merits of the business life as opposed to the life of an artist.

In the end it was Sarah, who had come to the United States at so young an age that she possessed no memories of Europe, who cleared the way for Aaron to go abroad. She had a sharp, no-nonsense kind of mind, but the fear that her husband knew intimately from personal experience was only a legend for her. The American Middle West, with its beauty and its bounty, had been the home of her youth and it had given her a sense of security and optimism that her husband could not know.

When everyone had had his say, Aaron recognized a

familiar look of understanding in her eyes and heard her say firmly to her husband: "The boy must have his chance. Let him try to do what he wants and we'll see what happens. After all, Aaron is still young enough to enter a profession if his ideas about a life in music do not work out." And financially there was really no problem. Aaron had saved a considerable amount of the money he earned working at the store. Putting it together with what his parents gave him, he would have ample means.

From that day on, impatience began to well up in him until he thought he would burst. Paris at last! Aaron felt that a part of him was already there. But first he had to conclude his studies with Rubin Goldmark.

Early in 1921 a large and rather elegant dinner party was held in honor of his teacher at the Hotel Esplanade in New York City. By now the students had all fallen into the usual categories—an inner clique, the "promising bright students" who faithfully followed their teacher's most cherished ideals, and the "black sheep" who insisted upon going their own way no matter how widely it diverged from hallowed ideals. Almost from the very first, Aaron Copland was the incorrigible who was in the forefront of the second group.

Frederick Jacobi, an "old boy," was given the privilege of escorting Mr. Goldmark to the gala affair and he also took over the responsibilities and pleasures of toastmaster. As the group finished their dessert, he rose and solemnly said: "You are now going to hear a performance of one of the best examples of a student's work—the harmonization of a chorale, in the Goldmark manner." A smile he couldn't quite stifle was then acknowledged by the rest of the group who were in on the fun.

As soon as the music began, the sharp dissonances and shocking harmonies told Mr. Goldmark that a little practical joke was being played on him. He went along with it like a good sport, expressing silent indignation and at the end of the piece he rose with mock anger and pointed his finger accusingly at Aaron as he said: "You're the culprit! *You* did it!" Everyone had a good laugh, especially Aaron, who was probably the only one present to enjoy the dissonance.

Now Europe, and especially Paris, drew closer with an astonishing reality as each day passed. Aaron Schaffer, an older friend who was now visiting Paris, kept stimulating Aaron's expectations with a series of eyewitness reports. Aaron was only fifteen when he had met Schaffer at a summer hotel. He said he was the first intellectual he ever knew, the first person he met who "talked the same language." Now Schaffer was writing: "I know you would find joy in this city if you were here; the concerts are simply countless and of every conceivable character." Aaron was gratified to know that Parisians shared his own passion for Debussy, assured by Schaffer that he is "one of the idols of the Paris musicians."

Soon Aaron would be hearing more of Debussy's marvelous music too, walking the same streets that he had walked, sitting in the same cafés. There would be the great museums to visit, and the French food he had heard so much about, and afternoon strolls along the banks of the Seine.

And then, suddenly, there was no time left for reverie. The days that had either fled by or dragged with such maddening inconsistency were now finished. There had seemed to be time enough for so many important things —certain friends to see, books to return to the library, clothing to buy—and then there wasn't time at all, for with an alarming and exhilarating suddenness the day of departure had arrived.

# 5

## The First Years in Paris

When Aaron Copland went to Paris in 1921 the city had become a beacon for artists, writers, and musicians throughout the world. The French capital had long had a tradition of intellectual freedom that had drawn the unconventional, the maverick, and the exile but now, more than ever, this was the city where new ideas were being born, where anything could happen.

World War I was over and with the cessation of destruction came a new surge of creativity. The map of Europe underwent drastic changes as the Austro-Hungarian Empire and Germany were forced to surrender much of their territory to the Allies. Several royal houses lost their power as democratic forms of government came into being, and many old traditions were being questioned and discarded.

With the defeat of Germany came a downgrading of things German, particularly in the world of music where it had long been the dominant force. The French composer Erik Satie voiced the attitude of French musicians when he said, "We want our own music, and if possible, without the sauerkraut."

There was a generally rebellious, defiant mood in the air that was forcing everyone, especially young artists, to search for new values and new forms of expression. Impressionism, with its subjective, sensuous images of the world, gave way to Cubism and Dadaism based on new, and to many, shocking, philosophies of art. Cubism, unlike Dadaism, was not opposed to reason. But its reduction of familiar objects to their basic geometrical forms horrified many art lovers who could not reconcile themselves to a portrait of a pretty girl represented only by straight lines, cubes, circles, and other basic shapes. Dadaism, which glorified the irrational, was the first antiart movement to appear. It preached nonsense and nonart and its declared purpose was to make clear to the public that all established moral and aesthetic values were meaningless—an attitude which obsessed millions of people at the end of World War I.

Impressionist music, which attempted to convey the essence of sensuous moods through richly varied harmonies and timbres, was now replaced by music that seemed dissonant and confusing.

Several attempts were made to give music a new dimension. Some musicians used new mechanical instruments, others were concerned with quarter-tone and polytonal music, experiments in jazz or unusual and bizarre combinations of instruments. The password was: try anything since anything is possible. Tradition counted for nothing, innovation and experimentation were of first importance.

Fortunately for everyone, the stage of this cultural free-for-all was France, where neither the memory of the war nor the extravagances of the nineteen-twenties were able to dim the French tradition of reason and a fine sense of balance. Perhaps it was this tradition that in the end helped produce so much art of enduring worth.

When the S.S. *France* sailed out of New York Harbor in the spring of 1921, the atmosphere aboard was one of high excitement and anticipation.

Long after the gay bon voyage parties of the morning's departure were over, the holiday atmosphere persisted. The sea wind and sun soon turned most of the passengers a deep tan, and the round of shipboard flirtations and parties began.

Amid all the gaiety, some serious friendships began to form. At Copland's table was a young Frenchman who spoke little English and didn't seem to want to learn more. He was more interested in playing chess with himself than in any other pastime. This was Marcel Duchamp, one of the leaders of the Cubist and Dadaist movements in painting; the artist whose famous work "Nude Descending a Staircase" had caused a scandal when it was first shown in America in 1913.

Duchamp was taken with the shy young American

who—he soon realized—was far more self-confident than he seemed. They became friends, and when Duchamp spoke about the Paris that he had known since childhood, Aaron listened with great interest. "You'll go to the Left Bank, of course," he told Aaron. "I know an excellent small hotel on the Rue de Seine that would be perfect for you. You can stay there more comfortably through the summer than anywhere in Paris."

"But I'm not going to be in Paris during the summer," Aaron protested. "I'm going to Fontainebleau."

"For heaven's sake why?" Duchamp asked with raised eyebrows.

"Well, you see," Copland explained, still unaware that he was confronting one of the great innovators of contemporary art, one who, in particular, despised existing traditions. "I'm going to attend a new school there. It's going to be in one of the wings of the Palace of Fontainebleau and Monsieur Vidal—Paul Vidal—is going to teach composition."

Duchamp's forehead wrinkled in disgust. "What a dreadful bore *that* will be! Why, it's nothing but a school of old fogies. Don't be a fool—there's only one thing to do and that's to remain in Paris."

Fortunately Aaron ignored Duchamp's advice. But the friendship continued throughout the voyage. Copland even brought forth a slight compliment from the Frenchman when he performed a Beethoven piano sonata at the ship's concert.

On the day of the announced arrival, at a sudden shout of "Le Havre!" everyone, that is, everyone except Duchamp, raced to the railing for their first glimpse of France. Aaron jostled with the others to get a better view and to watch the vague details of the coastline come into focus. But when he finally turned around to go below, there was Duchamp at his chessboard, expressing his disdain for the excitement of the Americans.

Aaron recalled reading about rugged French individualism. Duchamp was the first example of it he had encountered. As he went below to prepare for his last meal aboard the *France,* he mused about his friend's slightly eccentric behavior. Yes, there was no doubt about it, France was going to be a most interesting experience!

The confusion of disembarkation and customs, the swift, unintelligible flow of the French language all around him added to the excitement and intoxication of Aaron's first contact with France.

He found that the hotel recommended by Duchamp, along with most of the other hotels in Paris, had no rooms available. After several hours of looking, he finally found one almost too characteristic to be real. He was shown to a tiny room on the fifth floor where an old-fashioned bedstead, faded wallpaper, and a lingering smell of garlic helped to make this first day in France indelible in his memory.

But the disadvantages of the old Parisian hotels that make life miserable in the winter give them a matchless charm in the spring. Even the antique sink in a corner of the room, with not much more than a trickle of water, was not too bad. The bath had two disadvantages—it cost three francs extra and was two flights down. Aaron was prepared for this because already, in the early nineteen-twenties, the antiquated ways of French plumbing had become part of the European legend for American tourists. And to a young man about to see Paris for the first time, such things did not matter at all.

He dressed quickly, managed to make it clear to the taxi driver that he wanted to go to the ballet, and arrived just as the curtain was going up. It was a very good beginning for his first year in Paris.

After a week of sight-seeing, Aaron boarded a bus for the Palace of Fontainebleau, which takes its name from the town and is situated in the forest of Fontainebleau about thirty-one miles southeast of Paris.

The beautiful forest and lush countryside had attracted artists since the early years of the nineteenth century when Courbet and Corot first went out into the open to paint the landscapes which were to lay the foundations of Impressionist painting. Their interest in the effects of light inspired them to paint the luminous scenes of the placid woods and fields that were followed a quarter of a century later by the canvases of Renoir and Van Gogh which blazed with vivid light and color.

In the nineteen-twenties, the charming countryside was still popular with artists. Even such iconoclasts as Picasso found the idyllic pastoral setting inspiration for many paintings of the Cubist period.

To Aaron, whose life had been spent almost entirely in Brooklyn and who had traveled west of the Hudson River only when he went to summer camp, the grandeur of the palace and its formal eighteenth-century gardens were the revelation of a world he had only read about. In the week before school began, he spent many long hours wandering down the cleverly designed paths, admiring the precisely clipped hedges and rococo statuary.

He found a room with a French family and began to explore the lovely old town. The palace itself, with its tapestries and French doors that opened on broad terraces, created a setting that could not have been more appropriate for the study of eighteenth- and nineteenth-century French music. Aaron delightedly explored every corner of this beautiful old palace and grew especially fond of the comfortable, well-stocked library. Many of the books were sumptuously bound in leather with a large gilt "N"—a reminder of the days when Napoleon had been master there. Fontainebleau was Aaron's first taste of old French civilization and he wanted to see, and understand, a good deal more of it.

But the school itself was turning out to be a different matter. After only a few weeks had passed, Aaron was forced to realize that the quality of the instruction was not what he had hoped it would be. The class in composition to which he had looked forward so eagerly was especially disappointing. Paul Vidal, the instructor, had turned out to be a "French version of Rubin Goldmark but harder to understand because of the French patois he spoke." Copland's high school teacher at home had taught a distinctly school-book French and he was not prepared for Vidal's unfamiliar dialect.

Soon he found himself devoting more and more time

to studying French. He became friends with some of the students, explored the countryside, and studied French history.

Then, one day when his discouragement about his studies was reaching a particularly low point, a fellow student named Djina Ostrowska told him about a remarkable new teacher of harmony. "You ought to visit one of her classes," she suggested.

Aaron winced. "I was finished with harmony years ago," he replied, "and besides, how could a *woman* be a good teacher of composition? Name me one outstanding woman composer."

"Just come and see for yourself," Djina insisted.

Finally his curiosity got the better of him. He found a bright-eyed, eager-faced young woman enthusiastically explaining the harmonic structure of Modest Moussorgsky's opera *Boris Godunov*. She wore a long black skirt that came down over her low-heeled shoes; pince-nez glasses were perched on her nose. Altogether it was an appearance that really gave Aaron little idea of what a remarkable young woman she really was.

In later years he recalled that she had an "almost old-fashioned kind of womanliness about her." She also had a bright intelligence and a lively temperament which she brought into full play when she taught. She made Aaron see that harmony is one of the most fascinating aspects of composition. Even a primitive man could, and usually did, have a superb sense of rhythm. But harmony was by far the most complex aspect of composition and one that had developed slowly through the centuries. It was during Aaron's visits to Mlle. Boulanger's harmony class that he began to understand for the first time what an interesting subject the study of musical composition could be.

During the summer, when the class was invited to visit Mlle. Boulanger's country home outside Paris, Aaron was asked to go along. Apparently his charming manner and air of quiet determination had made a good impression. As he was not officially a pupil of hers, Aaron felt immensely flattered by the invitation. He came away from the afternoon feeling sure of the idea that had been growing rapidly in his mind since that first encounter— that Mlle. Boulanger was a unique teacher. More than anything else, he wanted to study with her. When he asked her to accept him as a student for the coming year, she agreed immediately.

Graduation day, if it could be called that after such a brief period of study, had come. It was a particularly hot day toward the end of August, so hot that most of the shops in the town were still shuttered tight against the intense afternoon heat. But at the Palace of Fontainebleau well-dressed guests were beginning to assemble in one of the great reception rooms. It was a smart gathering made up of students' parents who were vacationing in Europe, musicians, friends of the instructors, and—so it was whispered among the students—M. Durand, Debussy's famous publisher.

Only a few of the students had been able to prepare any new work. Much of the time they had spent in France had been devoted to observing and getting used to foreign ways. Paris, with the endless fascination of its streets and museums, its large international community, all took a great deal of time. But several students had brought scores that had been composed at home. Aaron's contribution was a short piano piece that he had written in New York, a work he called "The Cat and the Mouse."

Copland's performance was listed as one of the last works of the afternoon. He was sitting in one of the front rows so he couldn't study the faces of the audience as they responded to the works they heard.

But there was ample time to think about the summer that was now closing and also about his future in the world, especially his future in the world of music. His parents had agreed to one year of study abroad. Now that he was going to be studying with Mlle. Boulanger, he suspected that he would want to remain much longer than one year. Only the most absolute veto could keep him from learning as much as he could from her, no matter how long that might take.

Abruptly Aaron was jolted out of his reverie as the time came for him to perform. Somehow, the piece seemed just right for this program. It was brief, only five minutes long, and even though he had written it before he put foot in France, it had a witty, insouciant quality that gave it a kind of Gallic verve. It made liberal use of the dissonance that had horrified Rubin Goldmark. And already certain of the characteristics that distinguished much of Copland's future work were present— the qualities of precision, nostalgia, and a kind of "wiriness" that many critics heard in his work. When the piece was finished, the applause was loud and unmistakably approving.

Afterward, as the guests milled around tables loaded with iced orangeade and petits fours, Aaron was astonished to see M. Durand make a beeline for him.

"Monsieur Copland," he began, speaking in perfect English. "I must tell you that I was completely delighted by your little work."

Copland was suddenly at a loss for words. "Thank you," he said, getting out his handkerchief to mop a brow that was becoming very moist.

"What are your plans for the future?" M. Durand asked.

Surprised and delighted by M. Durand's interest, Aaron hesitated, but not for long. "I'm going to remain in France for another year. During the summer I did not study with Mlle. Boulanger but she has accepted me as a student for the coming autumn."

"Ah, that is good, very good," M. Durand said with a smile. "When you're settled in Paris will you come to see me? I'll have a contract prepared because, with your kind permission, I would like to publish 'The Cat and the Mouse.' "

Aaron was stunned. The first thought that entered his mind was the familiar image of the Durand music covers that had faced him for so long from the music rack of his piano. "The Cat and the Mouse" would now appear under the same cream-colored cover that enclosed the scores of Debussy!

The rest of the afternoon passed in a delightful haze.

Aaron had met Harold Clurman, whose brother had married his cousin, just before he left New York. They liked each other immediately and became lifelong friends. In the nineteen-thirties Clurman became one of the important directors of the New York stage and the guiding genius of the Group Theatre, a company that advocated the famous Stanislavski method. This theory of acting was later to be used with great success by the Actor's Studio, an offshoot of the Group Theatre.

When Harold Clurman arrived in Paris to study at the Sorbonne, it was decided that Aaron and he would share an apartment on the Boulevard Raspail. It was not far from the Rotonde and the Dome, two of the favorite cafés of the artists and expatriates living on the Left Bank. Within view of the terrace of the Dome, Rodin's statue of Honoré Balzac, the great French writer, had been placed with an unusual sense of the appropriate. Holding his cape around him, the noble figure seemed to brood loftily above the busy twentieth-century scene that swirled around him.

To be as much a part of life as Balzac had been—and yet to be able to give your inner vision form and reality—*that* was an achievement and one that Aaron thought about a great deal through the damp cold months that lay ahead. As November drew to a close, the heavy gray skies of the European winter gathered over Paris and life took on a definite routine.

Mornings were usually given over to piano practice. In the late afternoons there were scores to read and study. Once a week Aaron went for his lesson to Mlle. Boulanger's apartment and on Wednesday afternoons he would join her other students for a *dechiffrage* class, a general get-together for reading music. Occasionally one of the students would play a new composition.

Café life was important. Most of the cafés situated along the broad boulevards had large outdoor sections of tables that occupied much of the sidewalk space. In the summer they were adorned by potted plants and flowers and during the winter they were enclosed by movable glass walls. Most of the social life of the young students took place in these cafés. There was incessant talk, of course, but if you wanted to be left alone in the midst of the crowd, you could have that too. The cafés supplied writing paper and some people received their mail there. You could even do some work if you liked.

The high point of the week was the meeting with Mlle. Boulanger, who was to have a profound influence on Copland's musical future. In later years he described her as a woman who ". . . knew everything there was to know about music, pre-Bach and post-Stravinsky, and knew it cold. All technical know-how was at her fingertips; harmonic transposition, the figured bass, score reading, organ registration, instrumental techniques, structural analysis, the school fugue and the free fugue, the Greek modes and Gregorian chant."

But as the months passed and Aaron began to know her better, he realized that she was much more than a highly skilled and perceptive teacher of musical composition.

"She was," he wrote, "a continuing link in that long tradition of the French intellectual woman in whose salon philosophy was expounded and political history made."

Although musical aesthetics were the main topic of conversation at Nadia Boulanger's, few contemporary developments in the arts went unnoticed. Painters and writers such as Paul Valéry and Paul Claudel mixed with the musical great of Paris, figures of international fame such as Igor Stravinsky, Maurice Ravel, and others like Darius Milhaud and Arthur Honegger, who were just beginning to make their reputations.

Mlle. Boulanger was particularly fond of Paul Valéry. It was on the afternoons when he was present that the current literary scene would be given a lively discussion. Although few realized it then, the early nineteen-twenties were as momentous a time for literature as they were in the world of music. It was during these years that James Joyce's massive, unique novel *Ulysses* was published. This book was to change the course of literature, as was another masterpiece that was published in the same period, Marcel Proust's *Remembrance of Things Past*. Like much of the new music, these revolutionary books expressed aspects of human experience that had long been suppressed.

Copland read these books eagerly, as he did the work of Paul Valéry and André Gide. Many of Gide's pronouncements had great appeal for the young artists of the period. He wrote about the need to take things for what they are, the need to insist on being as one is. He acted on this philosophy in his personal life, and when he said, "One must dare to be oneself," he might have been speaking for an entire generation.

Aaron, like most of the other young people of the time,

thought a good deal about Gide's words and came to the conclusion that they offered good advice. But the important question was: "Which way to go about it is the best way?"

In music, unlike the other arts, the answer was sure and clear. Musical composition is one of the few arts in which there are few self-taught creators. It is essential that the aspiring composer have a firm grounding in the fundamentals, for without them there can be no real or enduring invention.

Painting and even literature have often been created by "primitives" or people with only a rudimentary grasp of the basic elements. But in music one must have the technical knowledge that is acquired with the study of harmony, structural analysis, counterpoint, orchestration, and score reading. The way was clear. If Copland was to "be himself," he must first acquire this indispensable knowledge.

# 6

# *Study with Nadia Boulanger*

As the year progressed, the bond between Mlle. Boulanger and Aaron grew closer. Each meeting increased his respect for her as an extraordinary teacher attempting what several famous composers have said was impossible —the teaching of advanced composition. Nadia Boulanger would probably have agreed that the truly inventive, deeply imaginative creator must have certain inborn qualities. But she was also convinced that every aspiring composer must be given a comprehensive understanding of the problems—and solutions—of composition that are a part of musical history.

Just as important as her technical knowledge was an almost instinctive sense of the way to guide a budding composer to maturity. She understood the anxieties and doubts that subtly delay and sometimes impede a student's progress.

To those who lacked the necessary talent, she made her feelings known without hesitation. But she could instill in those who had talent, and the will to develop it, an abiding sense of self-confidence.

Thus far, Copland had limited himself to two-page songs and three-page piano pieces. Like many young artists, he was apprehensive about attempting work on a larger, more complex scale. With Mlle. Boulanger's encouragement he began and finished a full-sized ballet— called *Grogh*—which lasted thirty-five minutes. Again and again, her confidence inspired him to begin work on a larger scale.

In 1925 Nadia Boulanger began to plan her first American tour as an organist. Although she knew perfectly well that Aaron had never heard an orchestra perform his work and had only "a nodding acquaintance with the king of instruments," she asked him to write an organ concerto for her.

"Do you really think I can do it?" he asked hopefully.

"But of course!" came the firm reply.

Mlle. Boulanger often spoke of *la grande ligne,* the long line in music. As Copland would return home through the soft gray dusk of the late Paris afternoon, the phrase would repeat itself in his mind again and again.

What exactly did she mean by *la grande ligne?* It was only after much pondering, and only in the last months of his time in Paris, that the full meaning of the phrase became clear to him.

Partly, Mlle. Boulanger was speaking of music that

flowed smoothly and with continuity. It was also what she spoke of as "the feeling of inevitability," that is, the feeling that all the parts "fit," that not even a small part could be omitted without the entire piece falling apart. But perhaps more than anything else, when speaking of *la grande ligne* she was referring to that intangible X factor in a successful creation of art—the elusive quality of unity that marks a work of art as a perfect whole.

Mlle. Boulanger was emphatic about one method of studying the art of composition. She never tired of telling her students: "Take the musical scores with you when you go to a concert or to the opera. Study the music as you hear it. Listen to the same work over and over again, until you know all of the music, every little phrase." Aaron came to the point where, if he found himself entering a concert hall without a score under his arm, he felt as though he were only partially dressed.

One series of concerts he never failed to attend was that known as the Concerts Koussevitzky. They were given each spring and autumn by Serge Koussevitzky, the famous Russian conductor who was to become, in 1924, director of the Boston Symphony Orchestra. He had a strong interest in contemporary music and his concerts were always exciting evenings, eagerly looked forward to by the musical intelligentsia and particularly by young composers who wanted to know what their contemporaries in foreign countries were doing.

As Koussevitzky was more interested in the work of young composers than the average conductor of his day, it was only to be expected that Mlle. Boulanger would arrange a meeting between Aaron and the great conductor who was about to pay his first visit to the United States.

When they arrived at Koussevitzky's apartment in the spring of 1923, Aaron, "with all the assurance of youth," had a recent score tucked under his arm. It was the "Cortège Macabre," an excerpt from the ballet Copland was working on under the guidance of Mlle. Boulanger.

After Aaron finished playing it, Sergei Prokofiev, who was also a visitor, suggested that there were "too many bassi ostinati" (repeated figures in the bass) present in the work. It was a good piece of criticism, as Aaron realized later on. Koussevitzky, meanwhile, was quietly weighing his words.

By offering to publish "The Cat and the Mouse," Durand had begun a fortunate chain of events in the summer of 1921. Now Koussevitzky added another link that was to lead to that most cherished dream of young artists everywhere—early recognition. When Prokofiev finished speaking, Koussevitzky announced that he liked the work and wanted to perform it during his first season as director of the Boston Symphony Orchestra.

Clurman and several other friends were informed of this good fortune over coffee in the Dome the following morning. They decided to celebrate with dinner at Les Halles, the great wholesale food market of Paris.

The news about Koussevitzky was as good a pretext as any other to celebrate, but generally none was needed to have a late supper at Les Halles. All through the night, while the rest of the city was sleeping, the whole area would bustle with activity as shipments of produce from the country came to market.

Often the wholesalers, dressed in heavy mufflers, berets, and overcoats, would light small fires near their stands, creating a theatrical scene that could easily have been the stage setting of an opera the students had seen just hours before. But unlike the opera, the market was fragrant with the rich odors of freshly picked vegetables, poultry, and fish, the great varieties of sausage and pâtés beloved by Parisians.

The restaurants of the quarter were famous for good, simple French food. Although they were primarily workingmen's restaurants, in the nineteen-twenties they became fashionable with artists and society people who often "finished off" an evening with a late supper at Les Halles.

That night, after a concert, Copland, Clurman, and a few others began their way to the market through the damp, narrow streets of the ancient quarter. While the others talked eagerly about the opera they had just heard, Aaron walked in silence, mulling over the strange musical experience that was *Pierrot Lunaire,* the revolutionary work by Arnold Schönberg that later came to be regarded as one of the great achievements of modern music.

Arnold Schönberg, the controversial Austrian composer who spoke of the "emancipation of dissonance," no longer adhered to the established laws of harmony. He created an entirely new organization of music which discarded the major and minor scales in favor of a method that is sometimes referred to as the twelve-tone system. Using this technique the order of the twelve pitches is fixed within a tone row. Subject to various manipulations this row, rather than traditional melody and harmony, becomes the basis of the composition, thus producing music that looks the familiar tonality which had been taken for granted. *Pierrot Lunaire,* one of his masterpieces, was called by Igor Stravinsky, "the solar plexus as well as the mind of twentieth-century music."

It was a work that was difficult to comprehend on first hearing but even with all its strange and disturbing dissonances, it seemed to Aaron that it was music of the first importance. He could see that the world of music would never be quite the same after *Pierrot Lunaire.* After walking in silence for several blocks, he turned to Clurman abruptly. "How did you like it?" he asked.

Clurman did not hesitate before answering. He too knew that he had just heard an extraordinary work of music. "I did!" was the emphatic reply.

Copland smiled. "Then you are one of us."

Schönberg's radical introduction of the twelve-tone method had made him one of the most talked-about figures of the nineteen-twenties. It was a departure of which Mlle. Boulanger did not thoroughly approve. But Copland, as a young student with an adventuresome, open mind, felt no need to disassociate himself from one particular school, or to ally himself with another. His musical ideas had already begun to change and he knew that they would probably change even more radically before he left Paris.

Aaron, who had been "all agog at coming to study in the country that had produced Debussy and Ravel," found that the former was rapidly losing his place in the musical hierarchy while the latter, as far as the avant-garde was concerned, hardly had any at all.

The scores of Maurice Ravel, with their dazzling timbre and controlled elegance, had been deeply admired by Aaron when he was still a student of Rubin Goldmark. And long before he arrived in Paris, he grasped every chance to hear the work of Claude Debussy that echoed, in such an enchanting and sensuous form, the light and shifting shadows of the Impressionist painters.

Debussy had written: "The primary aim of French music is to give pleasure . . . the musical genius of France is something like a dream in the senses . . . music must be free of all scientific apparatus. Music must seek humbly to give pleasure. Great beauty is perhaps possible within these limits."

But young musicians of the nineteen-twenties, busily engaged in polytonal and atonal experimentation, found these words quaint and old-fashioned. Polytonality is the use of more than one tonality simultaneously. Atonality, music without key or tonal center, was one of the new harmonic styles which Schönberg had introduced. These were the two most important movements which were taking music in a direction far from that advocated by Debussy. Leading the French opposition to Debussy's philosophy of music was Erik Satie and "Les Six"—the composers who more or less adhered to Satie's theories about music. They were Louis Durey, Germaine Taillefere, Francis Poulenc, Georges Auric, Arthur Honegger, and Darius Milhaud.

Erik Satie was a "most peculiar little old man who

worked in the daytime as a clerk in the post office selling stamps, and in the late afternoon and at night became a high and mighty potentate in the decisions of musical France."

He belonged to that curious group of artists who are great innovators with an extremely original viewpoint, but whose total creative work output is meager compared to that of their disciples.

Satie and "Les Six" produced music that aroused violent reactions from both the conservatives and the avant-garde. Virgil Thomson, who was later to become an astute American music critic, wrote of Satie: "His compositions are as simple, as straightforward as the remarks of a child. To the uninitiated they sound trifling. To those that love them they are fresh and beautiful and firmly right."

Jean Cocteau, who had written the libretto for Satie's famous ballet *Parade* was another advocate. With Ravel and Debussy in mind, he wrote: "Enough of hammocks, garlands, and gondolas. I want someone to build me music I can live in, like a house. Musical bread is what we want, music on which one walks."

Other writers saw in the work of Satie and "Les Six" less attractive qualities. These musicians were referred to as naughty children whose sarcasm and eccentricities were their main attributes. Some thought that they took pleasure in being as preposterous and outrageous as they possibly could. More conservative critics were quick to label this music, sometimes suggestive of sirens, typewriters, and dynamos, as an outright bid for publicity.

Copland made up his mind that the one thing he could not do was to make up his mind. Admittedly, some of the new work was difficult to listen to and even after several hearings refused to take any form at all. But other scores, such as Darius Milhaud's *The Creation of the World,* seemed, on the first hearing, to be an exciting work that would make a secure place for itself in the history of music.

For the most part, Copland reserved judgment on some of the shocking sounds of the time that were called, at least by their creators, music. In such a tumultuous era of flux and innovation there was only one thing to do and that was to listen.

There were many opportunities for listening as Aaron began to travel outside France, where he heard some of the great orchestras of Europe. In the summer of 1922 he visited Berlin. In 1923 he spent several months in Vienna.

Returning to Paris in the autumn of 1923, Aaron realized how swiftly his years abroad had gone by. After having agreed to one year of study in France, his parents had been persuaded to finance another year and then another.

More and more as news of old friends and of his family reached him, Aaron's thoughts turned to America.

Late in the autumn, Aaron sat at one of the tables of the Rotonde, waiting for Clurman and some other friends to join him for late afternoon coffee. The great plane trees that line the boulevards were shedding the last of their dry leaves. As Aaron watched the blue-smocked maintenance men sweeping them into an enormous pile in front of the café, he thought about the treeless streets of Manhattan, stark and ugly compared to the broad and leafy boulevards of Paris.

But New York had a different kind of beauty, although it was sometimes harsh and more difficult to enjoy. Aaron loved his native New York; he wanted to feel its excitement again. Yes, his mind was made up—he would definitely return home the following spring.

When Clurman arrived, the usual exchange of the day's events began. But Aaron could not keep his mind off the thoughts that had occupied him earlier in the afternoon. He almost felt that part of him was already in New York and that he was beginning to take his place in the musical life of the city. If there had ever been any doubt about the direction his future must take, it had now completely disappeared. He was not going to have the economic prospects of the young businessman or professional. And that was certainly going to be of concern to his parents who were perhaps still hoping that he had become more "realistic" about life. He would gently have to make it clear to them that only one path was right for him now.

It would certainly not be easy. Musical developments that had already become part of history in Europe were only beginning to be felt in New York. And the musical world, traditionally unreceptive to innovation, was far more straitlaced in New York than in Paris. In later years

*Benjamin Britten visiting Copland at Sneden's Landing, New York, 1949.*

*Aaron Copland listening to native musicians perform Brazilian drum rhythms in Recife, Brazil, 1941.*

A dramatic moment from Appalachian Spring. In the foreground, Martha Graham and Eric Hawkins; at left, May O'Donnell as the "Pioneering Woman," Washington, D.C., 1944.

At Tanglewood with Leonard Bernstein, Serge Koussevitzky, and Brazilian conductor Eleazar de Carvalho, about 1945.

*Aaron Copland and Carlos Chavez at an Inter-American Music Festival, Caracas, Venezuela, 1957.*

*Aaron Copland lunching with Thornton Wilder at New Haven, Connecticut, in 1948.*

*Aaron Copland with Virgil Thomson, Nadia Boulanger, and Walter Piston, after a concert honoring Nadia Boulanger, Washington, D.C., 1961.*

*At the White House after a performance of* Billy the Kid *for guests of President Kennedy. With Copland, choreographer Eugene Loring, producer Lucia Chase, and Oliver Smith, scenic designer, Spring 1963.*

# 7

# *Return to New York*

Soon after dawn Aaron was up and attempting to dress in his small cabin in the ship. For the six-foot young man it was always a discomfort to adjust to these cramped spaces. He moved quickly, as he usually does, and was soon up on deck, where he met a few other passengers who did not want to miss the unforgettable experience of the ship's entry into New York Harbor, one of the most spectacular approaches to a great city in the entire world.

It was a June morning and hot and humid but after breathing the stale air of his small cabin on D deck, it was good to stand at the rail and inhale the fresh sea air. Not talking much, the few passengers shared a quiet air of expectation. They had talked themselves out at a party the night before and already their thoughts were moving ahead to their day in New York and the various business and pleasures they must attend to. They gave themselves to the moment and watched the easy swoop of the gulls over the water as their raucous calls, now strong, now faint, floated out over the moist morning air.

Just outside the harbor, the ship cut her engines and the squat black tugs that were awaiting her took over the job of bringing the *France* to her berth in the Hudson.

Slowly the familiar landmarks began to slide by as the ship, passing The Narrows, moved beyond the Statue of Liberty, Ellis Island, and then into view of that sight that is at once terrible and beautiful—the skyscrapers of lower Manhattan.

After a joyful reunion with his family, Aaron began to call on old friends and see what changes New York had undergone since his departure. The fall of 1924 was a crowded, exciting time for him. He was at that momentous and critical time in a young man's life when his education is finished and he must find his place in the world he has chosen. For the artist it is a particularly difficult time and it was never less so than in the America of the nineteen-twenties.

Aaron was in exactly the opposite position of so many of the young people who were now converging on New York in search of artistic fulfillment and intellectual stimulation. For most of these young people—who had come from small towns all over the country—between the rich cultural life of New York and that of their home towns lay a vast gulf.

Aaron Copland, returning from the cosmopolitan art worlds of Paris, found New York arid and disappointing. It was inhospitable to innovation, whether it was home-grown or imported from Europe. Only a few years previously, the embittered Russian composer Prokofiev, after four years of struggle for recognition, had left New York in a mood of deep depression.

Aaron felt an even greater pang of homesickness for Paris when he realized more fully that the concert-going public in the United States was almost totally indifferent to contemporary music. And he knew that the time had come to face the hard fact that "in America, our new composers have been left to shift for themselves."

He recalled that Franz Liszt had concerned himself with almost every young talent in Europe that he happened to meet. Erik Satie had "played godfather to a whole brood of young Frenchmen. Braving ridicule, he even sought among high school boys for young genius." And there were others too, who had gathered around them the important young talents of their time—Casella in Italy and Busoni and Schönberg in central Europe. But in America there was absolutely no one who could shepherd the young generation of musicians into maturity.

Moreover, there was a fundamental difference in the attitude between the older generation and that of which Aaron was a member. As he saw it, "their attitude was founded upon an admiration for the European cultural tradition and an identification with it that made the seeking out of any other art formula a kind of sacrilege." He wrote that "the challenge of these traditions was not: can we do better or can we do something truly our own but, merely, can we do as well? Of course one never does, as well."

He was sure that to meet Brahms or Wagner on their

own terms one could never be better than second best. But it would be hard to convince these older American composers that the time had come to think in other musical terms. Aaron knew that the gulf between these two generations was certain to become wider.

Aaron could not very well put off any longer the problem of earning money. His parents had been exceedingly generous and he resolved that he would not ask them for another penny. But funds were dangerously low and the money had to come from somewhere.

In the nineteen-twenties there was really only one way for a young composer to make a living, and not a very good one at that. He had to teach, and if he wanted to make enough to eat, he couldn't afford to be selective about his students. The most reluctant, the little music haters forced to study because of ambitious parents—all had to be accepted.

This unappetizing prospect seemed inevitable but it was still several months away. It would have been easy to ask his parents for "just enough" to get him through the summer, but Aaron had made a firm resolution and he was determined to stick by it. When Abraham Ginsberg, an old friend from the Goldmark days, told him of an opening in a trio which was going to play at a summer resort in Pennsylvania, Aaron thought it sounded like a golden opportunity.

He saw a perfect summer stretching ahead—long leisurely mornings when he would be free to work on the organ concerto for Mlle. Boulanger (eventually called the Symphony for Organ and Orchestra), a pleasant luncheon served in the dining room, a few hours in the afternoon when he would have to play for the "tea dancing," and then a restful interlude before the dinner music, when he could read, nap, and write letters.

Things turned out very differently.

Within a hundred-mile radius of New York City are thousands of summer resorts that enter the highly competitive struggle to lure guests for the summer months. The Milford Inn had made a determined effort to build up a faithful clientele but the brightly colored brochures that gaily advertised delicious meals, modern bathrooms, and a crystal-clear lake "lovelier than Como" could not compete with the poor reputation the resort had made for itself the preceding summer.

From the very beginning, instead of the tinkle of crystal and silver and lighthearted laughter, an ominous calm lay heavy in the dining room. While Aaron and other members of the trio lunched in a corner of the almost deserted room, the proprietor, a charming Italian without a grain of business sense, hovered near the foyer graciously escorting the few guests into the dining room. But the strain of being charming for so long, while he knew that he was running in the red, began to tell after a few weeks. Soon there was to be a daily "practice period" for the young musicians.

This might have been an interesting interlude except for the fact that Mr. DiLorenzo was an impassioned opera lover who insisted that operatic excerpts be the main feature of the music program. He knew every note

of the major Italian operas and several of the more ob-
scure ones as well. They had been played in a particular
manner since the days of his childhood—in a provincial
town in southern Italy—and he was determined to hear
them played in precisely the same manner at the Milford
Inn.

To make matters worse, Mr. DiLorenzo now decided
to censor all performances. In a determined effort to
bring some liveliness into the deadly calm that seemed
to hang inexorably over the Milford Inn, he insisted that
the trio play only the joyful arias, the happy carefree
passages of the great operas. Not a note of *La Boheme*'s
sadness ever floated out over the dancing floor of the Inn.
Only the brief moments of joy—and usually those were
not sufficiently *vivace*.

"No, no," Mr. DiLorenzo would begin very calmly, for
he was really a very gentlehearted soul. "What is the matter? Don't you understand the word *vivace?* These musical terms are part of an international language. You
should understand *vivace!* With *life*. Play with feeling,
joy, *molto vivace!*"

Abraham raised an eyebrow in the direction of Aaron.
Aaron began to play.

After just a few bars, the interruption would begin
again. "What is the matter? Don't you understand my
English? I tell you, Americans are a wonderful people
but they don't understand opera! *Vivace* means with life,
joyous life. It must be happy, very happy. Now try again,
please."

Aaron raised an eyebrow in the direction of Abraham.

Abraham began to play. As the music continued, Mr. DiLorenzo's head tilted back and his eyes slowly closed. His head nodded slightly to indicate that an improvement had been made, but one that was slight and of no real consequence.

On the days when there were no "rehearsals," Aaron tried to work on the Symphony for Organ and Orchestra. By ten thirty most of the guests had finished breakfast and he went to the dining room hoping to find two quiet hours in which he could work. But this seemed to be the one time that the kitchen help felt free to sing, whistle, or gossip as they worked. To make matters worse, almost as though at a prearranged signal, plumbers or carpenters would appear with an excuse to begin pounding and sawing.

Finally, desperate for quiet, Aaron fled to the local movie theater and the curious piece of musical equipment that passed for a piano. He paid such a small fee for renting it that he realized it was pointless to complain about its poor quality.

There was a heavy odor of stale cigarette smoke in the theater and the floor was littered with the previous night's debris, crushed popcorn cartons, ice-cream wrappers, forgotten packages or gloves. But the important thing was the quiet that he now had.

In the meantime, letters had been flying back and forth across the Atlantic concerning Aaron's progress on the organ symphony. He *was* making progress, but not fast enough. The problems of adequate working space combined with the demands of Mr. DiLorenzo had not formed a happy background for this serious work. In fact, as the days went on, it seemed to be having the opposite effect. Suddenly Aaron decided to leave the Milford Inn and take refuge with his sister Laurine, who was now Mrs. Marcus, with her own home in Brooklyn. She would see to it that he had the right surroundings for composition.

Work went well at his sister's house and when the piece was finally finished and sent off to Mlle. Boulanger, Aaron began the search for a studio. He decided on an apartment at 135 West 74th Street.

He sent out cards announcing himself as a teacher. Then, with a satisfied sense of having done the right thing, he settled back and waited for the first timid student to appear. He realized that he might have to wait a long time for the really special student, the one that came eagerly and with great expectations, but he knew that it would be worth it.

Aaron was too realistic to expect an immediate response to his announcements. There were many teachers in the neighborhood who taught music theory, the principal fundamentals of harmony and counterpoint. Some of these had been well established for many years. Soon one week had gone by without an inquiry. Then another— and another.

But at least one anxiety had vanished. The score for the organ symphony had arrived in Paris and had been properly admired and praised. The work, Mlle. Boulanger wrote, ". . . is so brilliant . . . so full of music."

This made the steady silence at the door and telephone

somewhat easier to bear. Nevertheless, Aaron felt that efforts must be made to establish himself in the music community—and soon. He settled down to complete the orchestration of the Symphony for Organ and Orchestra and began to look up some of the people he had met in Europe.

Marion Bauer had been a visitor at Mlle. Boulanger's salon and had met Aaron there the previous year. She liked him, liked his work, and wrote to the League of Composers to let them know that a young man of enormous promise had come to town and deserved a hearing.

It was at the League's audition of his work, in Claire Reis's elegant 77th Street apartment, that Aaron met Paul Rosenfeld, the distinguished writer, lecturer, and music critic of the *Dial,* who was to become one of his most articulate supporters.

The men felt a deep admiration for each other. Aaron realized from the beginning that Rosenfeld was no ordinary critic, not simply a "detached bystander whose job may be considered finished when he has given the composer a casual hearing." Rather, he was the embodiment of Aaron's ideal critic, a man who ". . . is just as much a member of our musical civilization as any composer is. He ought to be just as serious when he writes his criticism as a composer is when he writes his music."

Paul Rosenfeld was all that, and more. Aaron wasn't the first unknown artist he had championed. Several years before, he had written enthusiastically about the neglected Charles Ives, and later he was one of the first critics to praise the fifteen-year-old Lukas Foss, who went on to become director of the Buffalo Symphony Orchestra.

Rosenfeld liked Aaron's gentle ways, that particular Coplandesque mixture of great self-possession and humility that has provoked so many admiring comments. Rosenfeld, in recalling the afternoon, wrote in the magazine *Modern Music:* ". . . at the keyboard, playing and singing one of his own compositions sways a slim, beglassed, shy and still self-assured young fellow with the aspect of a benevolent and scholastic grasshopper . . . swiftly there revives my delight in the fresh entirely individual sonorities . . . at last the composer comprehends our pleasure in him and his music. For the first time, he looks at us and openly smiles. It is Aaron Copland; still half boyish but a personality."

Claire Reis, founder of the League, was also impressed with the young composer. Not long afterward she suggested to Koussevitzky that Aaron be invited to join the League's board of directors.

"Please," Koussevitzky urged, "leave Copland alone until he is an integrated person. For a few years he should not give his energy to anything but composition."

Claire Reis decided to wait. When Copland finally became one of its directors in 1933, he "immediately became a real force. His influence and his judgment about works for performance as well as his advice about the magazine [*Modern Music*] were invaluable."

Meanwhile, Aaron looked forward to the forthcoming League concert. When it took place several weeks later, his work was well received and his name began to crop up in conversation among musicians. His financial problems continued, however; the doorbell remained silent. When not even one student appeared, Aaron began to wonder if he was destined to be a teacher after all.

Now his financial situation became really critical. And then, just when he needed it most, Minna Lederman, the editor of *Modern Music,* made Paul Rosenfeld aware of Aaron's situation. And through Rosenfeld's efforts, Mrs. Alma Wertheim, a well-known patron, agreed to sponsor him for one year. It was all that he needed to get down to serious work again. He was convinced that if he worked hard and well, the future would take care of itself.

# 8

## "It Seems Evident That in Five Years He Will be Ready to Commit Murder"

The Symphony for Organ and Orchestra received its first performance on January 11, 1925, at Aeolian Hall, with the New York Symphony Orchestra conducted by Walter Damrosch. In this first major composition some of the dominant characteristics of Copland's work are already apparent, particularly the combination of reflective tranquillity and boldness verging on stridency that is felt in so much of his work.

Aaron's family had come, of course, and many friends. They weren't sure of what they really thought of such strange, unfamiliar music, but when it was over they applauded loudly and heartily. The rest of the audience showed a moderate enthusiasm for the unusual new work and joined in the applause.

However, when it had quieted down, Walter Damrosch, instead of walking off the stage for the intermission, advanced toward the front, a handsome and respected figure. There was an expectant hush and after an appropriate pause to heighten the importance of his words, Damrosch said: "Ladies and gentlemen! It seems evident that when the gifted young American who wrote this symphony can compose at the age of twenty-three a work like this one," now another pause to heighten the tension, "it seems evident that in five years he will be ready to commit murder!"

Aaron and his relatives joined in the startled and embarrassed laugh that ran through the audience. Everyone accepted the shocking remark for the joke that it was, but the cutting undertone was understood immediately and an awkward few moments ensued. Then the intermission came to the rescue and in the confusion Aaron had time to think about Damrosch's little joke. Apparently the distinguished conductor had thought it necessary to make a kind of apology to the stolid conservatives in the audience. It made Aaron sad to realize that such apologies were still needed in what he had hoped was the enlightened year of 1925.

Meanwhile, Nadia Boulanger, who had arrived just in time to begin rehearsals for the Damrosch concert, was now trying to adjust to the frenetic pace of life in New York. Aaron was delighted with the idea of showing her the sights of the city. There was nothing of the expatriate about him. He loved New York as much as Mlle. Boulanger loved Paris. And although she made it clear from the beginning that sight-seeing would take second place to her many musical activities, Aaron was eager to get her reactions to a city as vastly unlike Paris as New York.

One night after a party, Harold Clurman and Aaron took her arm and firmly announced that the time had come when Mlle. Boulanger would see Broadway, which was admiringly called "The Great White Way" during the nineteen-twenties and thirties.

Broadway was loud, brash, and bursting with vitality and life. At eleven in the evening, as the three friends turned the corner of 45th Street above Times Square, they saw the usual surging mob of people that fills the area just after the Broadway shows have closed. There were thousands of people hailing taxis, rushing to parties or late suppers, sightseers gawking at the huge flashing signs, and at the corners, tight knots of figures that might have stepped out of Damon Runyon's *Guys and Dolls,* that story which told of lives with a theatrical background, lives that were a curious mixture of romance and vice.

Clurman was proud of New York and loved the theater district, where he now spent a great deal of his time. He turned to Mlle. Boulanger and asked, "What do you think of it?"

"It is *extraordinaire,* but not very raffinated," she replied with a touch of the Parisian snob.

Aaron and Harold roared with laughter because her unsure English only served to set off her foreign point of view. Later Clurman wrote: "We didn't think of Broadway's lack of refinement. We thought it was *extraordinaire.*"

Aaron thought that probably Boston would be more to her taste. He would find out soon enough, for the next performance of the Symphony for Organ and Orchestra was scheduled for performance by the Boston Symphony Orchestra a month later.

For a week prior to the Boston performance, the conductor rehearsed the orchestra with great care each day. It was said that "Copland walked on air." He found it hard to believe that Koussevitzky should lavish so much attention on an unknown American youth. Actually it was not out of character, for Koussevitzky had long been one of the world's foremost champions of contemporary music. Although Aaron had met the famous conductor in Paris, he hadn't had a chance to learn much about him.

Serge Koussevitzky's fame as a musician had begun long before he instituted the Concerts Koussevitzky in Paris. He was born in Vishny-Volotschok, a small town in Russia, where his father made his living in part by playing the violin at weddings. Poor and unknown, but talented and charming, Koussevitzky made his way to Moscow, where he was finally allowed to enroll at the Conservatory.

From the beginning he was a brilliant student. He met Tchaikovsky and participated in small musical gatherings at his apartment. Before long he was a virtuoso of his chosen instrument, the double bass, largest of the string instruments and familiar today as the one that generally carries the beat in dance combos. Within a few years Koussevitzky was head of the bass section of the Bolshoi Theatre Orchestra and a member of the faculty of the Conservatory. The village boy had now acquired a dignified bearing, wore impeccably tailored clothes and a luxurious moustache.

Things seemed to be moving along very well but soon they were to move even better. At a private musicale he met the immensely wealthy Natalya Konstantinova, whom he soon married. Now new resources allowed him to perfect himself in the art of conducting, where his extraordinary talent and imagination came to the fore.

He formed a publishing house with the primary aim of encouraging young composers. Alexander Scriabin, skimping along in Lausanne, was one of the first to benefit. Not satisfied to stop there, Koussevitzky set up a special fund of five thousand rubles to help composers in need. To his roles of virtuoso soloist, conductor, and publisher, he now added that of patron—and the legend of the *grand seigneur* began.

His great dream was to bring music to thousands of people who lived far from cities and rarely, if ever, had a chance to hear well-performed orchestral music. With this idea in mind, he arranged a tour of the Bolshoi Theatre Orchestra down the Volga River that attracted worldwide attention. To accommodate the orchestra and his party he hired a vessel which resembled the old Mississippi riverboats of the last century.

Later on, when the Russian revolution made the pursuit of this way of life impossible, the Koussevitzkys moved to Paris, where the conductor, now famous throughout Europe, inaugurated the distinguished Concerts Koussevitzky that had been one of the great musical experiences of Aaron's first years in Paris.

However, the change to American life—when Koussevitzky took over the directorship of the Boston Symphony in 1924—was not a particularly easy transition for the conductor and his wife.

There was not a large musical audience in Boston in spite of the city's long support of a symphony orchestra that was one of the finest in the country. The orchestra was maintained by and for the educated and wealthy elite, and when Koussevitzky took charge, the situation was much the same as it had been for generations. This highly conservative society did not relish the prospect of having their aesthetic ideals shaken, and they certainly did not care to be exposed to the disturbing and unpleasant noises that Serge Koussevitzky called music. It was many years before Bostonians fully recognized the true stature of their new conductor.

Now Aaron Copland was finding that his work was esteemed in the eyes of such a distinguished and renowned musician. Before long Koussevitzky was commissioning new works and calling Aaron by the affectionate Russian nickname of "Arosha." And when the patricians of Back Bay temporarily forgot *noblesse oblige* and began to hiss Aaron's work, Koussevitzky remained a staunch and steadfast admirer.

Unfortunately, the music critics too reacted unfavorably. As Koussevitzky had seen almost from his arrival, he could expect no help from the conservative press in educating Boston audiences. Rather, they would have to be put down for some postgraduate work in musicology themselves.

Nothing moved Koussevitzky's steadfast belief in Aaron Copland. And Aaron, as he gradually came to understand the depth of the conductor's knowledge of music, learned to trust the older man. Many years later he wrote, "I have never met a man who loved music more passionately than Serge Koussevitzky."

# 9

# *The MacDowell Colony and Return to Europe*

Aaron Copland's meeting with Koussevitzky was perhaps the most fortunate and important which he was ever to have. In America, the *grand seigneur* continued to serve his almost compulsive need to promote, foster, and spread the gospel of modern music. But he believed that in America—unlike Europe—the range of talent was extremely limited. In fact, in later years he admitted to the belief that when he first arrived in this country in 1924, he found that "American music was barely alive." Copland's work was a marked exception.

Aaron was in need of someone who was not only perceptive enough to recognize burgeoning talent, but a man who also had the courage, prestige, and power to stand behind his convictions. Koussevitzky had all this and a dash of Russian genius besides. When Aaron Copland appeared on the scene writing music that was intoxicatingly new and alive, Koussevitzky immediately recognized his talent and dedication and determined that his work would be heard.

That week of rehearsals with the conductor in Boston had kindled the creative fires more than anything else could have done at this point in Aaron's life. He was eager to begin a new work that Koussevitzky had commissioned for the League of Composers after the conductor had heard the Symphony for Organ and Orchestra. When Paul Rosenfeld suggested that he might find the seclusion that he needed at the MacDowell Colony in Peterborough, New Hampshire, Aaron decided to investigate.

He had been hearing about the MacDowell Colony since his return from Europe and hoped that sooner or later he too would probably be one of its privileged guests.

It was one of the first such colonies of artists in the United States, a place where every effort was made to provide an atmosphere conducive to creative work. During the months that he was there he could forget entirely about the financial problems that plague most artists throughout their lives.

The establishment of such a colony was the wish of Edward MacDowell, whose home the colony had once been. He belonged to the same generation of composers as John Knowles Paine, George Chadwick, Arthur Foote, and Horatio Parker, men whom Aaron Copland considered "overgentlemanly, too well mannered. . . . Their culture," he said, "reflected a certain museumlike propriety and bourgeois solidity." But unlike these other nineteenth-century composers, MacDowell had a strong original talent. "His music," Aaron wrote, "shows more independence of spirit, and certainly more personality than was true of his colleagues around 1900." In 1925 MacDowell's name was better known, and his music more frequently played, than that of any contemporary.

But when the youthful Copland arrived at the Colony, he was highly critical of MacDowell's work—as the young generally are of the preceding generation's accomplishments. Later he realized that "MacDowell had a sensitive and individual poetic gift, and a special turn of harmony of his own."

MacDowell and his contemporaries were a frequent subject of conversation between Aaron and Roy Harris, another young composer who was in the midst of creating some interesting new works.

There were several writers at the Colony and some poets and sculptors. For the first time, over meals and during long pleasant evenings around the fire, Aaron met many different kinds of artists whose interests were in fields that he had not had time to study. Among the other people working there were the poets Louis Untermeyer and Elinor Wylie, and the writer William Rose Benét, all of whom acquired distinguished reputations in later years.

Although self-discipline in matters of work had never posed a problem for Aaron, he was drawn to the definite, fixed routine that was established in such creative centers as the MacDowell Colony. He liked the sense of going

to work every morning at exactly the same time and seeing the same faces across the dinner table in the evening.
Lunch was brought to the individual studios so the artists
could have a day of completely uninterrupted work if
they wished.

"Sometimes it produced results," Aaron said, "and
sometimes it didn't." And if it didn't, if the morning's
work was unproductive or sterile, it didn't seem to disturb
him. By now he was familiar with that ebb and flow in
the creative process and he knew that fertile periods are
inevitably followed by those which are more or less
fallow. On mornings when it was difficult to get down to
work he would remember the maxim of the Russian composer Igor Stravinsky that ". . . just as appetite comes
with eating, inspiration comes with working."

Occasionally artists who are working in such close
proximity to other creative people feel overshadowed and
confused by so much creative activity going on around
them. Aaron's basic self-confidence and assurance saved
him from such a problem. He liked to hear the contro-
versies that raged over the aesthetic problems of the day
and he said that the more he was exposed to different
ideas and "had a chance to bat them around," the more
he knew what his personal convictions were.

Aaron was deeply engrossed in a work which was to
be an important turning point in his career, a major work
destined to become a familiar title in the repertoires of
many leading symphony orchestras throughout the country. The main problem he had set himself was to see
what he could accomplish by giving jazz a formal symphonic treatment.

He made good progress on the new composition commissioned by Koussevitzky and took it to the conductor.

For Aaron—as for most other composers—taking a score to Koussevitzky for the first time was an ordeal. Generally, Koussevitzky's reaction was instantaneous and effusive. If he liked a new work it meant a performance by the Boston Symphony Orchestra, an "exhibition" that would be as perfect as any young composer could possibly hope for. If Koussevitzky did not like the work, perhaps another conductor would. But every composer knew that the performance would be without the "special atmosphere" that surrounded a Koussevitzky premiere.

In later years Aaron wrote that "just as every ten-year-old American boy dreams of being President some day, so every twenty-year-old American composer dreams of being played by Koussevitzky."

The conductor was enthusiastic about the new work, which Aaron called *Music for the Theatre.* He scheduled it for a performance on November 20, 1925, and having a keen practical as well as visionary mind, he made sure that Aaron included a bill for the final score and parts so that the composer would be fully compensated for all his expenses. This established a precedent, for until this time American orchestras paid royalties to European composers for the performance of their works but refused to compensate American composers. It was this discrimination which Koussevitzky now began to combat.

*Music for the Theatre,* a suite in five parts for small orchestra, is considered by some musicians to be among Copland's best works. Because he wanted to write a work that was "specifically American in character," he incorporated strong jazz elements that were then an important part of the American scene. However, it was unusual to hear jazz in a serious orchestral work and the piece shocked many audiences. *Music for the Theatre* was an important, controversial work of its time, and today still retains its youthful exuberance and enthusiasm.

The title is perhaps misleading, for Copland did not intend the music to be a part of any theatrical production. Perhaps the name came from his concept of the music as the kind of sophisticated glittering musical entertainment that one associates with a large city's places of amusement.

Whatever the reasons for the title, its choice was a masterstroke. Titles often have an almost magical significance, particularly in the realm of music or abstract art where the viewer or listener seeks some clue that will lead him to familiar ideas in the real world.

It is likely that from this point on, Aaron Copland's name was associated with theatrical works in the minds of many, especially those persons who would need new scores for their theatrical productions whether in ballet or films.

Within fifteen years Aaron Copland was to become one of the world's most accomplished writers of music for the theater.

In March 1926 Aaron and Harold Clurman returned to Europe for a five-month visit. They had a busy schedule ahead of them. For the first part of the summer Aaron would participate in a concert of American music to be given by the Societé Musicale Indépendente in Paris. He planned to attend the International Festival of Contemporary Music at Zurich after the concert was over, and then spend the rest of the summer in a small town in the Pyrenees. The mountains that divide France from Spain are a favorite summer refuge for artists in that part of Europe.

The first stop was Paris, where they were soon visiting the Boulangerie (bakery), as both detractors and admirers of Mlle. Boulanger had labeled her salon. It was there that Aaron met the young musician who was to become an important friend in later years.

Roger Sessions was born in Brooklyn but brought up in New England. Aaron described him as ". . . by nature a perfectionist. Every work signed with his name is sure to be the result of extraordinary care, perhaps exaggerated meticulousness . . . in general, Sessions makes the impression of a philosopher-composer rather than a composer pure and simple."

Because of these qualities, Sessions' work never became as well known as Aaron Copland's, but in the world of music he is regarded as one of the country's most gifted composers. Now, at Nadia Boulanger's salon, the two young men gossiped about recent musical events at home and resolved to see each other when they returned to the United States.

Aaron was eager to go on to the music festival at Zurich. Once he was there, however, the lighthearted mood of the summer began to change. One of the main works of the program at Zurich that summer was Arnold

Schönberg's Quintet for Wind Instruments. For Aaron it was not only a disappointment but an "outstanding failure." It seemed a work that was "nothing but the principles and theories of composition leading to complete aridity." He remained skeptical even after Anton von Webern, one of Schönberg's disciples, assured him that "there was no more reason to expect to appreciate this quintet on a single hearing than to understand Kant after a cursory perusal."

Aaron and Harold decided to finish the summer with a quick visit to Germany. The two young men had found out that as well as being devoted friends, they were also excellent traveling companions for each other. Aaron was fond of Harold's sudden enthusiasms and Harold liked the quiet strength, the gentle yet firm assurance that Copland possessed.

For both young men the name Germany conjured up memories of Hansel and Gretel, the magical mythology of the north and those delicious Christmas sweets of *Lebkuchen* and marzipan. Together, they looked forward to visiting the dark fragrant pine forests and the storybook towns with gingerbread houses. And for a few days the dream seemed to be coming true. The roads through the Black Forest were filled with strong, tanned hikers with rucksacks on their backs. The streets in the villages were scrubbed and clean and the peasant women in the marketplaces were appropriately picturesque as they exhibited their fat geese and heavy sausages.

But in the larger towns there was a different atmosphere. All through the day they noticed an excessive activity in the streets. The Nazi movement was rapidly gaining momentum in Germany at that time and Aaron and Harold could sense the electric response of the people everywhere.

Intense nationalism—an attitude that ran contrary to Copland's temperament—was finding virulent expression in the Germany of the nineteen-twenties. In the Reichstag elections of 1928, Hitler's National Socialists would suddenly gain much power, and by 1930 emerge as a major party beginning a reign that culminated in World War II.

Now, in 1926, there was something ominous in the way the brown-shirted Nazi troopers swaggered through the towns. They were crude and easily given to brutality. With a sense of foreboding, Aaron and Harold decided to leave Germany immediately. Aaron's next visit to this country was to be in some respects even more alarming.

# 10

# *Jazz Comes of Age*

An article in a 1921 issue of the *Ladies' Home Journal* bore the title "Unspeakable Jazz Must Go," yet it looked as though jazz had come to stay for a long, long time. Aaron Copland had heard the exciting new syncopations of jazz when he was in his early teens, at about the same time that the general public was becoming aware of this first truly American music. Irving Berlin wrote "Alexander's Ragtime Band" in 1911 and a few years later W. C. Handy wrote the "St. Louis Blues." These songs were among the first important works that were responsible for the beginning of the jazz craze that began to sweep America about 1915.

Aaron often heard snatches of the songs as he walked the streets of Brooklyn and on special occasions he was allowed to go to the brash, lively vaudeville shows that were in their heyday. But most of the time it was in his friends' apartments that he heard the exciting, pulsating jazz rhythms which made such a lasting impression. Many of Copland's most important works of the nineteen-twenties made extensive use of the jazz idiom.

Although jazz was gaining enormous popularity every-where, there was still a wide gulf in 1915 between jazz and anything that might be called music by most of the music lovers of the time. In the nineteen-twenties Ameri-can jazz bands made long and highly successful tours abroad. In Europe, serious composers began experiment-ing with the new jazz forms soon after the first performers arrived. This was particularly so in Paris, where mu-sicians were in open rebellion against the aesthetic estab-lished by the Impressionists. During his first years in Paris, Aaron was astonished to discover the high respect with which so many cultured people regarded jazz. The Russian Igor Stravinsky noted the touching dignity of the New Orleans jazz funerals and was one of the first to mine the rich new source of inspiration. He wrote "Piano Ragtime" and "Ragtime for Eleven Instruments" using strong elements of jazz in both works.

Darius Milhaud made extensive use of the new jazz forms in one of his greatest works, *The Creation of the World*. And Jean Cocteau, after hearing a performance of jazz with dancers, described the reactions of the audi-ence which "gave them a standing ovation, torn loose from its reserve by that extraordinary spectacle—which is to Offenbach's foolishness what a tank might be to a horse-drawn carriage, vintage 1870."

Most American composers began to think of jazz seriously only after the Europeans had recognized its value. The reason, of course, was that composers in this country were still too culturally insecure and used to following the European tradition to see the musical riches in their own back yard.

By 1923 and 1924 it had become fashionable to listen to jazz throughout the United States. Some liked it raw and hot; others were more interested in what was being called "symphonic jazz." The exciting rhythms that were so dance-provoking were called, in the slang of the period, "peppy" and "snappy." An entirely new kind of musical verve came into being with the use that jazz made of such instruments as the saxophone and the banjo.

As a young man entering his twenties, in the nineteen-twenties, Aaron Copland caught the spirit of the times and was swept along in the current. He often went up to Harlem late at night, to such places as the Cotton Club, where jazz was played in an atmosphere that aimed at attracting downtown audiences.

Copland was fascinated by the particular timbre of the jazz band, the special tonal color that exists partly because of the absence of strings, with the exception of the banjo. In later years Aaron described how deeply impressed he had been by hearing ". . . the extraordinary rhythmic attack of the best brass sections, the unusual timbres produced out of thoroughly familiar instruments, and the general spirit of freedom and unconventionality surrounding a first-rate band."

Many people went to Harlem in search of what they

called "primitive music" and musicians such as Duke El-
lington gave them just that. Part of the fun was watching
and listening as the men in the brass section made their
horns "growl and moan with a bloodcurdling effect."

Meanwhile, in downtown Manhattan new efforts were
being made to promote a different kind of jazz. In 1924,
Paul Whiteman organized "The First American Jazz
Concert" in New York's Aeolian Hall. Whiteman was an
excellent popular musician and jazz entrepreneur. He
wanted to give this music a greater respectability by
bringing it the prestige it could get only in a concert hall.

Perhaps to suggest some of the new sounds that were
going to be heard, the stage had been decorated with
frying pans, some other tin utensils, and a trumpet. For
some inexplicable reason two Chinese mandarins looked
down at the audience from their perches atop their tall
pillars.

But however garish the decor, this first jazz concert
was one of the most exciting and notable events of the
season and one which attracted many distinguished musicians.

Jascha Heifetz was there. Sergei Rachmaninoff, Ernest
Bloch, Leopold Stokowski, and many others of the musical elite had come to see exactly what Paul Whiteman
had in mind when he announced his "educational concert." Certainly one of the events which made the evening
memorable was the first performance of George Gersh-
win's "Rhapsody in Blue."

Aaron Copland was amused to hear how many conversations on music dealt with the question of the "seri-

ousness" of jazz. In later years he expressed some of his feelings on the subject by writing in *Our New Music:*

> "I'm afraid that it is too late to bother with the question since jazz, serious or not, is very much here, and it obviously provides pleasure. The confusion comes, I believe, from attempting to make the jazz idiom cover broader areas than naturally belong to it. Jazz does *not* do what serious music does either in its range or emotional expressivity or in its depth of feeling or universality of language. (It does have universality of appeal, which is not the same thing.)

Copland believed that basically jazz had only two really vital expressions—either the "blues mood or the wild, abandoned quality so dear to the youth of all ages."

He found this emotional range limiting, but was excited by the technical aspect of the jazz rhythms which could easily be applied to other musical styles.

One of Copland's first works to make deliberate use of jazz was *An Immorality,* with a text by the poet Ezra Pound. The work is scored for women's chorus and a piano accompaniment. With the chorus singing in contrapuntal style and the piano beating out its jazz polyrhythms, the effect achieved is one of hot jazz that oddly recalls music of the fifteenth century.

Copland thought that Europeans had really only toyed with jazz and quickly abandoned it. He knew the results would be vastly different in the hands of an American composer, and many of his important works of the following years—such compositions as *Music for the Theatre,* the Piano Concerto, and the *Symphonic Ode*—bear out this belief. During this period Copland's determination to relate this music to the world around him became an almost obsessive idea.

He summed up his attitude and its origin when he wrote many years later in *Music and Imagination:*

> In France, where the characteristics of French culture are evident at every turn . . . the relation of French music to the life around me became increasingly manifest. Gradually, the idea that my personal expression in music ought somehow to be related to my own back-home environment took hold of me. The conviction grew inside me that the two things that seemed always to have been so separate in America—music and the life about me—must be made to touch. This desire to make the music I wanted to write come out of the life I lived in America became a preoccupation of mine in the twenties.

Although the preoccupation itself became less important as the years progressed, Copland's music continued to reflect the experience of a creative artist aware of the unceasing flow of modern life around him.

# 11

## *Composer in Manhattan*

During the last years of the nineteen-twenties there was a restlessness in the air, an acceleration of life that almost verged on hysteria. The objective of living, so it appeared, was the exclusive pursuit of pleasure and fun—and the faster and more intense the better. "Red-hot" jazz pianists were the heroes of the day. Parties were not thought a success unless they were wild and lavish and didn't really get started until all the rugs were picked up so the guests could Charleston freely from room to room. These were the days of the booming stock market, the flashy Ziegfeld's follies, and of F. Scott Fitzgerald, the gifted writer who brought the jazz age alive in many of his novels and short stories. After Henry Ford introduced his mass-produced, low-priced cars, the public suddenly realized that a fast new means of transportation was

86

within the reach of almost everyone. The impulse to quick change was reflected in the real estate market, especially in New York City where the skyline was rapidly changing. Much of the character of the city was altered during these years when sections such as Greenwich Village, once cheap and attractive to artists, became fashionable and more expensive.

Aaron was happy to return to the city in the fall of 1926. The summer in Europe had not been a productive one and those last days in Munich had left a painful memory that was not helped by news reports from other recent travelers to Germany.

After his return to New York in October, Aaron took a new studio at 123 West 78th Street. It was not to be satisfactory for very long, because early in his career he had discovered that his best hours for composing were the night hours between 8 P.M. and 2 A.M., when there was no danger of interruption. "Music is largely the product of the emotions," he said once with a touch of humor, "and I can't get emotional early in the day."

But neighbors seldom approve of music in the small hours of the night. He had to move from one place to another and wherever he went there were indignant protests. One night as he worked on the Piano Concerto there came a violent knock on the door.

He tried at first to ignore it. When finally he opened the door a large, fierce-looking man pushed his way in and strode to the piano. Copland had visions of ivory keys and broken strings flying around the room. Instead, the man only peered in. "What I want to know," he said belligerently, "is how you make the left hand go. I can get the right but not the left."

The unexpected turn the situation had taken appealed to Aaron's sense of humor, always a strong part of his personality. His easy graciousness soon put the fellow at ease. After an amiable chat, Aaron went back to work on the Piano Concerto.

But the interruption had somehow broken the flow of ideas. After trying to work for another hour without making progress, Aaron decided to give it up and take a walk.

It was one of those marvelous winter nights in Manhattan described by so many writers who have lived there. Aaron stood for a moment in the doorway, breathing the cold dry air as he pulled on his fur-lined gloves and tightened his scarf. Around him was the crisp, silent radiance of the city after a deep snow. Then, with that curious sense of being in a strange, enchanted place—a feeling well known to New Yorkers in winter—he stepped out in the streets of what is probably the most materialistic city in the world.

The snow was almost ankle-high. In doorways and stairwells that would have exposed garbage, assorted debris, and trash cans in summer, a heavy, glistening coat of new snow concealed every trace of ugliness. The wind was cold but not cutting, the snow so fresh and clean, Aaron decided to take a long walk to mid-town. He crossed Central Park, a silent white world of blue and white crystal, while admiring the sharp black silhouette of the skyscrapers against the dazzling winter sky.

At Fifth Avenue he decided to walk toward Fifty-Seventh Street where the shop windows, bulging with luxury goods for Christmas, were arranged with an artistry that is equaled in few other cities of the world.

Paintings gleamed from richly ornate frames, highly polished furniture was shown in exact period settings; he passed window after window full of brocades, crystal, and perfume. At Bergdorf Goodman, every mannequin wore a sumptuous coat of rare and expensive fur.

The sounds of the Piano Concerto ran in his head as he moved through the quiet, deserted streets. He would be showing the score to Koussevitzky in just a week and he felt a certain mild anxiety which he quickly pushed away. His beloved New York was having one of its most magical moments, at one of the most magical times of the year. He returned home exhausted and yet refreshed. He regretfully saw that it was three o'clock in the morning and too late to work. Somewhere, somehow, he *had* to find a studio where he could work throughout the night, if he wished, without interruption.

Aaron now traveled frequently. He was always eager to leave the city and he could easily imagine the pleasure of spending much more time abroad, perhaps a full year or two in London or Paris. Yet he knew he would feel a sense of relief and gratitude when he found himself home again.

Sometimes this need for New York seemed mad and unreasonable, as mad as the city itself could often be. The articulate French architect Le Corbusier had called

New York a beautiful and worthy catastrophe. Without a doubt, it could be uglier than any other great city; parts of it were filthy. The climate was terrible, the politics unbelievably corrupt. And yet, just as it was a distillation, a concentration of man's most sordid materialism, it was also the distillation of the finest that he could produce. In New York could be found the best music, theater, painting, publishing, the highest pitch of luxury, as well as of artistic and intellectual achievement.

Aaron finished the Piano Concerto in the late autumn of 1926 and Koussevitzky scheduled it for a January 28, 1927, performance in Boston. Aaron's parents went to attend the premiere. Now retired, they were proud of their youngest son who had won such an important place in the world of modern music. But their knowledge of this world was limited and they were bewildered and upset when Aaron brought them the first reviews of the concert. It was painful for them to read in the *Boston Transcript:*

PIANO CONCERTO—COPLAND THE OGRE
PLEASURE, PLAUDITS, DERISION, WRATH
Mr. Koussevitzky—Takes a New Way
"That Terrible Concerto"

Philip Hale, critic for the *Boston Herald,* wrote: "If this Concerto shows the present condition of Mr. Copland's musical mind, he is on the wrong track . . . we found little to attract, little to admire, much to repel. . . . The [work] also shows a shocking lack of taste, or proportion."

The *Boston Post* gave a yet more acid review. Quoting Copland to the effect that "you couldn't read a program into the [Concerto] if you tried," the critic reported that "with no effort at all the listener visualizes a dance hall next door to a poultry yard. . . ."

As a young artist by now used to such bitter words, Aaron Copland was not seriously disturbed by the reviews. He tried to explain to his parents why the critics wrote as they did, and to make them understand that none of this had any real bearing on the central issue of his creative life—his great need and pleasure in music.

Aaron tried to cheer them up by telling them of how many of the great artists had been subjected to cruel, unfair criticism. If he were going to continue to grow and produce, an artist had to view such attacks with the utmost detachment. He left them in a better frame of mind and began a letter to a friend: "I went to the mirror to see if I could recognize myself . . . when the Concerto is played again ('O horrid thought!') we must see if we can't get the police to raid the concert hall to give a little added interest to this 'horrible experiment.' " In New York, the Piano Concerto was played again by the Boston Symphony.

Although it is played without any interruption, the concerto is really divided into two contrasting parts which are linked thematically. The first movement is slow and lyrical; the second, very fast and rhythmic. Both moods of jazz are used—the slow, poignant blues and the "snappy," rhythmic one.

Instead of the hissing and laughing there was careful listening and warm, but sparse, applause. It would have startled many in the audience to hear Oscar Thompson, music critic of the New York *Sun,* state, fifteen years later, that he considered Copland's Piano Concerto the most impressive symphonic work in the jazz idiom by an American or European composer.

"It is melodious," he wrote, "it is fluent and it has a driving force. That the composer . . . should subsequently have lost his faith in the idiom as a basis for art expression is significant, since no other serious composer had accomplished so much with it as he did in the Piano Concerto."

But Aaron had now come to the conclusion that he had said all he could say in the jazz idiom. The time had come to move on to new musical ideas.

Aaron was now happily established in a loft studio which solved the problems he had had with neighbors. It was in a building on West 63d Street, where Lincoln Center for the Performing Arts now stands. He had managed to stay afloat financially through most of the nineteen-twenties but there were still periodic financial crises. He faced one of these in 1927 when the fellowship which he had been awarded by the Guggenheim Foundation in 1925 was about to expire. He was weary of looking for grants or patrons.

Paul Rosenfeld was about to give up his position as lecturer at the New School for Social Research in New York. He recommended Copland as his replacement. At that time the New School was perhaps the leading liberal educational institution in the country and a center for many of the newest developments in modern thought. Typical of the trend it followed was its pioneering lecture courses on psychoanalysis. Aaron Copland found the atmosphere much to his liking and settled down to a routine of lecturing and concert organizing that was to last for ten years.

The commissions which radio was beginning to give young composers were another source of income. The major networks had just been formed—the National Broadcasting System in 1926 and the Columbia Broadcasting System in 1927. Keenly aware of the vigorous new force of radio, they did much to encourage the writers of serious music.

In 1929 RCA announced a competition for a new symphonic work by an American composer. The prize was an unprecedented $25,000—enough money to make many young men move quickly to their pianos and pens. Aaron planned to enter his *Symphonic Ode,* a large orchestral work which was still unfinished. He worked feverishly, knowing there was still a vast amount of work to be done, but trying at the same time to convince himself that he would be able to finish it. He worked steadily through the following weeks but realized with a sickening feeling about a month before the close of the competition that it would be impossible to finish it in time.

Still, he knew he could not afford to let such an unusual chance go by. One afternoon, almost in desperation, he remembered *Grogh,* the ballet he had written years ago in Paris that had never been performed. He began to develop it and discovered, to his joy, that the work went easily, perhaps too easily. But when it was finished, he felt that he had accomplished something that he could submit without any regrets. Now in the form of a suite of three dances, he gave it the title of *Dance Symphony* and sent it off.

The judges felt that none of the work submitted warranted the full $25,000, so they broke it up into four awards—$5,000 each to Copland, Louis Gruenberg, and Ernest Bloch, and $10,000 to Robert Russell Bennett, who had submitted two compositions.

Since the $25,000 had seemed such an incredible sum to begin with, there was no feeling of disappointment or loss. Aaron was grateful to get the $5,000; that would more than keep him for another year. By careful planning, he actually found that he could make it last for two years.

When the *Symphonic Ode* which he originally planned to submit to the RCA competition was finished, it presented more problems. Koussevitzky had agreed to perform it but was distressed about the difficulties in playing the composition. He said the orchestra had spent several hours in rehearsal and still could not play it. Then he suggested that if Aaron would change the rhythm indications (the 2/4 plus 6/8 section to 5/4) the problem would be solved. In 1930 the combination of 2/4 and 6/8 was not as familiar as it became in later years.

Aaron laughed at the idea that it was difficult to play. "There is nothing to it," he told Koussevitzky, "the rhythm is an easy one to play."

But Koussevitzky knew what he was talking about. He

immediately replied: "Come on up to Boston, take over the rehearsal yourself and you'll see how 'easy' it is. After an hour's rehearsal, we can play only three bars," he jokingly concluded.

Since Aaron was reluctant to make any change in the score, he decided to go to Boston to attend the rehearsal. Koussevitzky turned the orchestra over to Aaron and left the hall. Aaron had only to conduct for a few bars when he immediately realized that he was wrong and agreed to make the change.

The *Symphonic Ode* has been called one of the most compelling and distinguished works Copland produced during this period. Now he was beginning to rid himself of the "composers' paraphernalia"—the arpeggios, fill-in sonorities, and similar devices of some of the earlier works. There are still jazz elements in the *Ode* but a new note of austerity can be heard, one which was to lead to the starkness of the Piano Variations. Considered within the framework of Copland's entire output, the *Symphonic Ode* is an important, pivotal work.

One important critic had only hostile words for the *Ode*. Laurence Gilman, of the New York *Herald Tribune* —who had previously been one of Aaron's most fervent supporters—wrote:

It was my pleasure and privilege to praise Mr. Copland's widely execrated Piano Concerto when it was played five years ago. But in comparison with that gusty and joyously challenging work, the new Ode is, for the most part, impotent and unrewarding . . . hearing it, one visions Mr. Copland lost in agonizing lucubration, praying Heaven to make him Hard and Stripped and Sharp Edged and Astringent and all the other things that a composer must learn to escape the sin of sensibility.

The dedication page of the *Ode* reads: "To the Boston Symphony Orchestra—Serge Koussevitzky, Conductor, on the occasion of its Fiftieth Anniversary."

Commenting on the *Ode,* Copland said: "I regard it as one of my most important works. I tried for something; I tried hard; and I feel that I succeeded in what I attempted."

# 12

# *Journeys to Paris*

Copland's fondness for Paris and French life, which he had come to know intimately during the early part of the nineteen-twenties, kept drawing him back to Europe again and again. The visit with Clurman in 1926 had only increased his deep feeling for the city and its stimulating intellectual life. He returned again in 1927, 1929, and 1931.

But he was no longer simply an observer of foreign life or a student. His lectures and reviews of contemporary music in various periodicals were well received in the United States. Now he was to begin reporting from Europe, especially for the League of Composers' respected magazine *Modern Music.*

For several months he had been eagerly looking forward to Igor Stravinsky's oratorio *Oedipus Rex,* for which Jean Cocteau had written the text. It was one of the works which Aaron intended to review.

Although Stravinsky's reputation was becoming more brilliant with each passing season, it had not been so long ago that he had suffered hearing members of the Vienna Symphony Orchestra whisper among themselves that the *Rite of Spring* was *schmutzige musick* (dirty music), or that he had had to cope with what he called "open sabotage" at their rehearsals. All this was painful but perhaps easier to bear in view of the fact that Stravinsky had first heard his detractors call the work the "Massacre of Spring" after its first performance.

But this composition was only one of several triumphs that Stravinsky had brought off in the years between 1909 and 1921. His scores for Diaghilev's Ballets Russes, especially *The Firebird* and *Petrouchka,* had been greatly responsible for the incandescent reputation of the ballet that spread throughout the world.

Aaron, who was to have a lifelong admiration for Stravinsky's work, later wrote that "heading the list of Stravinsky's original gifts was his rhythmic virtuosity. Nothing like it had ever been heard in Paris . . . it was Stravinsky who revitalized our rhythmic sense. He gave European music what amounted to a rhythmic hypodermic. It has never been the same since."

Copland was very impressed by the score for *Oedipus Rex* and its influence seems to appear in some of his own compositions of the following years. In his review for *Modern Music* he described the work as "a new, impersonal approach to music."

While he was in Paris, Aaron ran into Roger Sessions again and together they chatted about *Oedipus Rex* and many of the other exciting theatrical and musical events taking place that spring. Sessions was a rather serious and solemn young man whose highly individual viewpoint Aaron found stimulating. They visited some of the favorite places they had come to know during their many previous visits, enjoying the incomparable loveliness of the Parisian spring.

While exploring some of the haunts of the early days in Paris, they visited Shakespeare and Co., which Sylvia Beach had made famous as the publishing house of James Joyce's *Ulysses*. Shakespeare and Co. was primarily a bookshop; it was only on rare occasions that Miss Beach actually ventured into publishing. An eccentric sharp-faced woman who usually dressed in mannish clothes—a man's hat, a man's bow tie, and velvet jacket—she had an extremely perceptive eye and was devoted to the fostering of new literary talent.

It was at her shop that Aaron saw Ernest Hemingway, who was then at work on some of his early brilliant novels. He was usually chatting with Miss Beach in her office at the rear of the shop, a kind of inner sanctum where the favored gained entry to chat, to get information on new arrivals, and to browse through some of the literary curiosities that Miss Beach had collected. Among the most interesting were some original manuscripts of Walt Whitman's, roughly scribbled on the backs of envelopes that were now dark and yellowed.

Copland and Sessions enjoyed visiting Shakespeare &

Co., as they enjoyed their other leisurely activities in Paris. Yet their conversations often turned back to the grim realities of a young composer's life in the United States. It was during these hours together that they realized their ideas about the immediate future of modern music had taken a parallel course.

They agreed that the situation in which American composers now found themselves was thoroughly disheartening. A number of younger American composers had achieved reputations abroad before they were accepted in the United States.

And certainly no one could be expected to go on writing music that would not be played. No matter how indifferent or reluctant the general public was, both young men agreed some way must be found to give new music a hearing. Without it, no composer could be expected to grow and develop toward more mature work.

The time had come to take action, and the sooner the better. It seemed clear that if no one else was going to arrange more concerts of contemporary music, they would have to do it themselves! In 1928, the fruit of these talks came into being when the Copland-Sessions Concerts announced its first program.

There was much talk in Paris about Ezra Pound, the expatriate American poet, whose interest in new musical ideas had caused him to "launch George Antheil," the American *enfant terrible* of the nineteen-twenties, who calmed down in later years and produced film music that was neither very interesting nor very important.

Antheil had written a work he called the *Ballet Mécha-nique*. It was planned for an orchestra of sixteen pianos wired, synchronized, and operated from a central control. The music was to be magnified through several loud-speakers.

Ezra Pound believed that music should be taken out of the concert hall and made a vital part of industrial life. He saw the whole clamor of a great factory rhythmically regulated "not to a deafening din, but to a superb sym-phony." Perhaps, he reasoned, the factory manager could be the musical conductor, with the workers the instru-mentalists. This was, after all, simply an extension of the methods of sailors and primitive workers who instinc-tively make an effort to harmonize their natural work rhythms.

Music, Pound said, was the art most suited to express the fine quality of machines that were coming to be an in-creasingly important part of modern life. He believed that, musically speaking, George Antheil was showing the way.

In the art galleries along the Rue de Seine, on the Left Bank, Dadaist artists were exhibiting startling new works which they claimed were an enlightening commentary on society and art. There were strange assemblages of tools, old plumbing fixtures, and many other unrelated objects of modern life which, in their new juxtaposition, were supposed to reveal a new aspect of reality.

Neither Copland nor Sessions found any of this new work very interesting or amusing. But they continued to look at it and to talk about it. Perhaps this was a part of its purpose—its function as a spur to keep the senses keenly aware. But they realized that the old standards of art could certainly not be used in evaluating Dada, just as many of the accepted ideas about dissonance in music had to be discarded in trying to comprehend the new work of the time. In any event, the Dadaist creations were perhaps a fitting climax to the eccentricities of the decade.

In the early spring of 1929 Copland made plans to return to Europe once again. He left for Paris in May, only four months before the stock-market crash that was to change the course of almost everyone's life. Aaron's main objective was to arrange a concert of contemporary music which would give Parisians a representative hearing of North America's most "advanced" composers. The five were Virgil Thomson, Roy Harris, Israel Citkowitz, Carlos Chávez, and Aaron Copland. With the exception of Carlos Chávez, all the men had been pupils of the increasingly famous Nadia Boulanger.

She helped arrange the program and did her best to see that the concert was well attended. Luckily, Serge Koussevitzky, who had just come to Paris to conduct Modest Moussorgsky's opera *Boris Godunov,* gave the press an interview in which he had high praise for the American musical scene. It was a complete about-face from his views of 1924 when he first arrived in the United States.

He now stated emphatically that America had the most intense musical development of any country in the world and led in the appreciation of good music. "A phenomenal musical renaissance is in progress in the United States," he said, "Americans have the active temperament which (contrary to the opinions of many) has been the salvation of America's artistic development. They have stimulated orchestral development, just as they have created immense business enterprises. The American people have an inordinate genius for growth." Stating that Igor Stravinsky was the most outstanding influence in modern music in America, he named Aaron Copland, Roger Sessions, and John Alden Carpenter as the most promising composers.

Coming at this particular time, Koussevitzky's words were the best publicity the Americans could possibly hope for. The concert took place in the elegant Salle Chopin on June 17, and was well performed and warmly applauded. But the French critics would not for many years be able to view the American arts as anything but rather crude and negligible efforts. They were united in their disappointment with the concert; the only work to which they gave any praise was Aaron Copland's Two Pieces for String Quartet.

Back in the United States, where the economic depression was deepening with each passing month, Aaron found it necessary to be more frugal than ever. With careful planning he would make his RCA award last as long as possible, and he felt that he could still afford another trip to Europe—one which was to be his last for many years. He was interested in returning to Germany where the *Gebrauchsmusik* movement was gathering momentum, the term meaning "music for use."

There were two basic forms which the *Gebrauchsmusik* took: the first was the development of music for amateurs to perform: operettas and cantatas for school children, instrumental pieces for school and college orchestras, and works in which the audience participates by singing some of the choruses and songs. The second was music for performance by professionals but intended for a wider audience. This was the vast amount of incidental music that was now coming into being because of radio and films—music which would have a specific function and, at the same time, "political and social significance for a changing world."

In Germany *Gebrauchsmusik* often took on a bitterly satirical character because of its acid commentary on modern society. One example of this, which Aaron was eager to see and hear, was Kurt Weill's *Die Dreigroschenoper,* or *The Threepenny Opera*. He also wanted to hear more of the German composer Paul Hindemith, whose reputation was beginning to spread abroad. In the spring of 1931, together with the young musician and writer Paul Bowles, Aaron again set off for Europe.

They stopped briefly in Paris to pay their respects to Nadia Boulanger and went on to Bilignin (near Grenoble) to visit Gertrude Stein and her friend and secretary Alice B. Toklas in their French country house.

Gertrude Stein's highly unconventional approach to literature resulted in writing that was primarily concerned with the associations and sounds of the words themselves.

It was this emphasis on sound—and the variation of a verbal theme—that placed her in the forefront of writers who have strived for certain effects in literature which were previously found only in music.

Aaron was impressed with Miss Stein's qualities of strength and determination and found her "a definite presence." Both she and Miss Toklas were deeply involved in French life but still in need of constant injections of stimulating news from the United States. As they all went driving around the countryside to visit friends, Aaron noted the old French reluctance to accept an outsider, no matter how Francophile the individual might have become. After living for thirty years in France, she was still "Miss Stein." As the afternoon wore on, Aaron took pleasure in the usual French courtesy but noted a strong undercurrent of reserve toward the Americans.

On the way home they all chatted about Aaron and Paul's plans for the remainder of the summer. Their idea was to go to the French Riviera, a plan which horrified Gertrude. It was a dreadful mistake, she said. The Riviera had changed drastically in the last few years and was turning into a splashy, vulgar carnival. She strongly recommended another place that was still largely unknown to Americans, unspoiled and exotic—Morocco.

Aaron and Paul decided to take her advice and left soon after for Africa. Once there, Miss Stein's suggestion backfired, at least for one of the two young travelers. Aaron couldn't work, felt constantly ill at ease, and looked forward to leaving. Paul Bowles found Arab culture and society so much to his taste that he eventually made Tangier his permanent home. Gradually his interest in music was superseded by his talent for writing, and in later years he produced several interesting novels based on his unusual experiences in Arab society.

In December, Aaron went to Berlin where Ernest Ansermet, conducting the Berlin Symphony, had scheduled Copland's Symphony for Organ and Orchestra.

Again he stepped into an alien and hostile environment. Berlin, he felt, was possessed by an atmosphere of growing unrest; it had a quality of impending doom that was being increased by growing unemployment and taxation. Germany was full of bands of jobless wanderers, some of the German youth "which had been robbed in the war, starved in the blockade, stripped in the inflation—and which now, with no money and no beliefs . . . sprang like a breed of dragon's teeth waiting for its leader."

Aaron felt oppressed by the endless rows of gray apartment houses with their identical smells of decay and sauerkraut. It was difficult to see how the restaurants managed to stay in business at all with their menus that offered little more than watery lung soup or boiled horseflesh.

One bright memory remained of this trip—the meeting with Christopher Isherwood, the young English writer with the boyish lick of straight blond hair and the bright, staring, intense blue eyes that recorded so much of the chaotic world around him in his novel *The Berlin Stories,* later to be the basis of the successful Broadway play, *I Am a Camera.* Aaron also met the girl who was Isherwood's model for the enchanting and outrageous character of Sally Bowles.

Aaron, who never drinks hard liquor (and is also a nonsmoker), had to pass up tasting the original concoction that she called "Prairie Oysters," a dangerous mixture of whiskey, raw eggs, and Worcestershire sauce. The girl's light chatter and her sense of fun were a welcome counterpoint to the tension and anger in the streets. Nevertheless, it was good to return to New York, even the New York of 1931.

# 13

# *The Bitter Years*

Although Aaron had been hearing reports of the deteriorating economic situation in the United States, he was not prepared for the widespread despair he found upon his return from Europe.

After the stock-market crash in late 1929, economic conditions grew steadily worse until 1933, which was perhaps the most bitter period of the depression years. Millions of people found themselves without jobs or the hope of getting any. Breadlines became a familiar sight and food stamps were issued by the government for the very poor.

Suddenly an intense national self-scrutiny began to sweep the country. The nation had never before undergone such a period of self-analysis and introspection. Soon the artistic climate began to reflect this questioning and the despair and search for new values that accompanied it.

There had been some forerunners of this important change even in 1928, the year that the French writer André Gide, turning from his doctrine of personal liberation at any price, published *Voyage au Congo,* a revealing and often shocking book on the injustices of the French colonists in the Congo. Gide's reputation and influence were growing and this, and other works, found a wide audience whose interest was beginning to focus on the larger problems of society. During this period of the nineteen-thirties, the problems of the individual became secondary; those of society were of first importance. Everywhere artists, writers, and musicians were shifting the focus of their aesthetic views and their immediate objectives. They believed that the search for individual expression, which had fascinated so many people in the nineteen-twenties, was really immature, selfish, and unrealistic in view of the immense changes that were taking place.

For the time being, as young intellectuals talked excitedly about social injustice and the rise of dictatorships, music became less important for many young people.

Some writers began to think of themselves as leaders of the new American proletariat. Men such as the famous American poet Archibald MacLeish, who had spent most of the nineteen-twenties experimenting with the ideas of the French symbolists ("a poem should not mean but *be*"), now turned their attention to America and its heritage that had yet to be assessed. What was this America? According to Archibald MacLeish:

Americans were people who had the luck to be born on this continent where the heat was hotter and the cold was colder and the sun was brighter and the nights were blacker and the distances were farther and the faces nearer and the rain was more like rain and the mornings were more like mornings than anywhere else on earth—sooner and sweeter and lovelier over unused hills.

Look around, the poets said, not only at who and what you are but at the wonder of *where* you are. Again and again the cry was taken up. The young American writer William Saroyan also spoke of the need to recognize the here and now, but with a different emphasis. In the preface to his first book, *The Daring Young Man on the Flying Trapeze,* he wrote: "Try as much as possible to be wholly alive, with all your might, and when you laugh, laugh like hell, and when you get angry, get good and angry. Try to be alive. You will be dead soon enough."

There was a wide revival of interest in historical figures such as General Grant and Mark Twain. Carl Sandburg wrote his monumental volumes on Abraham Lincoln. America, America—at long last Americans were discovering their own country, remembering the vast and wonderful continent that they had forgotten about for too long.

Soon they were writing about it, painting it, celebrating it as never before. They explored the old folktales and ballads, exhumed such famous historical figures as Daniel Boone, and Davy Crockett. For the first time American folkways, the regional tales and legends, became respectable and even fashionable. People began to take a second look at their rusty butter churns and colonial furniture, and museums belatedly realized that American arts and crafts had a place in their exhibition halls.

Musicians were slower to voice their reactions, but before long they too had joined the movement that insisted art must concern itself with the problems of society.

In 1933 at the second Yaddo Festival—a series of concerts which Copland arranged on the Trask estate Yaddo near Saratoga Springs, New York—Roger Sessions warned that the American composer "must end his isolation and get in touch with current musical activities in general, especially the phase of musical education which concerns the public as a whole." Not so long before that, Paul Hindemith in Germany had expressed the same idea when he said: "It is [regrettable] that . . . so little relationship exists today between the producers and consumers of music. A composer should write today only if he knows for what purpose he is writing. . . ."

Hindemith was speaking as a composer of *Gebrauchsmusik,* the "music for use," of which Copland had heard memorable examples during his last trip to Germany. Now, in the chaos and flux of the depression years, his thoughts turned again and again to the function of music in the modern world and his contributions to that music.

Copland had made a reputation as one of the most imaginative and original composers in the country; he was an established and respected figure in the world of music. But he was dissatisfied and deeply disturbed by the prospect of continuing to write music that would be heard by only a very small section of the population.

Now, as American painting and literature were beginning to speak to the common man in terms that he could understand, music should certainly follow. And Copland reasoned that it *had* to follow if it was to play an important part in the new America that was to rise from the present chaos and dissolution.

The immense changes brought about by the advent of the radio and phonograph also influenced Copland's attitude toward the kind of music he wanted to write. Both of these important inventions made music available to millions of people whose entire musical experience had been limited, in some cases, to listening to a country fiddler. Now they could tune into Bach's *Brandenburg Concerti* at the flick of a dial. During the middle nineteen-twenties the new developments of electrical recording vastly increased the quality of the phonograph record. Ernest Newman, the respected music critic of the London *Sunday Times* wrote: ". . . until lately it was a little difficult to take even good orchestral records quite seriously . . . but all at once however it seems gramophone recording has taken an enormous step forward . . . at last an orchestra sounds like an orchestra."

Copland's thoughts often turned to these great masses of people who would now be hearing orchestral music for the first time. Later on, summing up these thoughts, he wrote in *Music and Imagination:*

During these years I began to feel an increasing dissatisfaction with the relations of the music-loving public and the living composer. The old "special" public of the modern music concerts had fallen away, and the conventional concert public continued apathetic or indifferent to anything but the established classics. It seemed to me that composers were in danger of working in a vacuum. Moreover, an entirely new public for music had grown up around the radio and phonograph. It made no sense to ignore them and to continue writing as though they did not exist. I felt it worth the effort to see if I couldn't say what I had to say in the simplest possible terms.

For most Americans, the economic crisis was growing more grave with each passing day. There were hundreds of applicants for every job, and more and more families broke up their homes and moved in together in order to save rent money. In the meantime, these early months of 1931 that were bringing tragedy into so many lives were bringing Aaron Copland more prestige within the music community.

The *Dance Symphony* (which does not involve any actual dancing) was performed on April 11 at the Academy of Music in Philadelphia, with Leopold Stokowski directing. The symphony was well received. Perhaps the catcalls and hissing were now fading into the past. As a matter of fact, there seemed to be a new trend in effect— louder clapping and emphatic approval from the more musically enlightened members of the audience.

In January of this year the *Piano Variations,* one of Copland's major works, had received its first performance at a League of Composers' concert, with the composer at

# PIANO VARIATIONS

the piano. It is a work which gave expression to the same fierce emotions that so many writers were displaying in their new books.

Some critics said that the work spoke of the thousands of alienated, homeless men now taking to the road. Others were reminded of the music of both the Negroes and the Jews, both dispossessed people who are symbols of uprootedness. The elements of Copland's work to which they referred were the ambiguous thirds, sixths, and sevenths of the Negro blues as well as the declamatory leaps of Jewish synagogue music.

The moods evoked by this work change swiftly from the fierce and angry to the naïve, warm, and tender. The characteristic Copland note of austerity is sounded throughout, a distinctive quality that finds many different expressions in his entire output. Wilfred Mellers, the perceptive and articulate English critic, wrote that out of these "multifarious elements" Copland had created a work of "austere but humane nobility." Further on, he noted ". . . the steel girders within which Copland so miraculously discovers a human warmth." And still another critic called the *Piano Variations* Copland's "most uncompromising piece and perhaps his most original."

The *Variations* is an excellent example of Copland's celebrated "economy of means." It was this ability to discard all the nonessentials, to concentrate on the central kernel of an idea, that Paul Rosenfeld had commented on as early as 1929 when he wrote that "the earmark of Copland's music is leanness and slenderness of sound." In the years that followed almost every critic commented on his ability to achieve the maximum effect with the most economical means, the transparency of his textures and the absolute precision—one of his favorite words—of his tonal vocabulary.

The lonely, meditative character of the *Variations* was strongly felt by many listeners. Among them was the dynamic young American dancer Martha Graham. She had always been "attracted to the idea of the theme and variations," and when she heard Copland's work she responded to its "wonderful, strange vitality." Not able to get it out of her mind, she finally called him and asked his permission to choreograph a dance to the music.

Aaron raised his eyebrows and with his characteristic look of wry amusement replied, "But how can you dance to *that?*"

Martha Graham convinced him that she could, and the result was a difficult solo dance, lasting about thirteen minutes, which she called *Dithyrambic.*

In the early part of 1933, one of the blackest periods of the depression years, Aaron's inherent optimism and ebullience finally gave way. Compared with many of his friends and relatives, his position was fairly secure. He had no responsibilities, no obligations to a family that prevented him from coming and going as he liked. What he could not do was to stem the mounting wave of deep sadness he felt for these people who were involved in the most tragic experiences of their lives.

During these months Harold Clurman, now director of the ambitious, progressive Group Theatre, had arranged for the entire company to spend the summer at their country headquarters called Green Mansions, a beautiful, heavily wooded place about fifteen miles north of Lake George, in New York. When Aaron was asked to join them for the summer, he jumped at the chance.

Here was an opportunity to be with a group of young theater people who were weathering the frustrating and discouraging times with more bravado and hearty spirits than the ordinary artist could muster. They could always find some good excuse for a party and Aaron Copland loves parties. In fact, as Leonard Bernstein said many years later, "Aaron loves parties more than any man I know."

Aaron quickly packed some summer clothes, the score of *Statements for Orchestra* and, with a great sigh of relief, left a New York that was now a city of unbelievable misery and despair.

Work on *Statements* proceeded slowly. The work was commissioned by the League of Composers for performance by the Minneapolis Symphony Orchestra, whose conductor was Eugene Ormandy. In the program notes Copland wrote: "The title of 'Statements' was chosen to indicate a short, terse orchestral movement of a well-defined character, lasting about three minutes. The separate movements were given suggestive titles as an aid to the public in understanding what the composer had in mind when writing these pieces." These titles are: Militant, Cryptic, Dogmatic, Subjective, Jingo, and Prophetic.

When Ormandy performed the work on January 9, 1936, he played only the last two movements. Copland continued to work on the composition off and on, and it was not until six years later that the full orchestral version received its premiere by the New York Philharmonic Orchestra under the direction of Dimitri Mitropoulos.

At Green Mansions Aaron worked a part of each day on Statements but found himself impatient to join the group at meals and during their long and often heated discussions. Harold Clurman encouraged these intellectual free-for-alls because he was firmly opposed to any ivory tower concepts of art, or art intended for the special individual or the elite. Clurman was an ardent humanist as well as a man of the theater and he placed a strong emphasis on art as it related to society. Inevitably, the political ideologies of the time came in for their share of intense argument. Aaron thrived on these discussions and applied much of what he heard to his own ideas about the new forms that music must take. He was still writing music that had an esoteric quality, but his mind was gradually moving toward new musical ideas that would reach millions of people.

During these years, the public's interest in modern music was at the lowest ebb Copland had observed since his first days as a young musician. Definite action had to be taken, some way found that would give living composers the hearing they absolutely must have if contemporary music was to survive.

Partly, of course, Copland wanted to find audiences for his own music, but he was also deeply concerned about the work of the many dedicated and talented men writing music that deserved attention. Then, as in later years, he felt there was something wrong, even ominous, about a society that was not interested in the music of living men.

Recalling that "Les Six"—the group that gathered around Satie—had made a far greater splash in the world of music by functioning as a unit rather than as separate individuals, Aaron began to mull over the idea of an American group which would be bound together by certain mutual objectives. The common ground need only be now, as then, a passionate belief in living contemporary music and a firm determination to see that music played and sung, and also criticized and talked about. For only by the mutual involvement of the professionals and the listening public could musical life be established as a vital part of contemporary society.

Now Aaron's innate ability to organize came to the fore. This, together with his equanimity and ability to deal with volatile artistic temperaments, enabled him to initiate and guide this and many other group activities. He approached some of the young composers who might be interested and was delighted by their immediate enthusiasm for the idea. The alliance was formed with the name the Young Composers' Group. Its members were Paul Bowles, Henry Brant, Israel Citkowitz, Lehman Engel, Vivian Fine, Elie Siegmeister, and Arthur Berger.

In this group, as earlier with the Copland-Sessions Concerts and later with the League of Composers, Copland acted as creative adviser and also did a great deal of administrative work. No matter how difficult and absorbing might be the problems of his own composition, he always found time for these groups whose one aim was to expand the world of modern music.

# 14

## *Mexico*

In the early nineteen-thirties Mexico was an ideal refuge for artists, writers, and musicians who wanted to live abroad but could no longer afford to make the more expensive trips to Europe. Also, during these years in New York, few events of musical importance took place in the summer months. The young musician who was interested in keeping up with the latest developments could easily go away at this time and still feel that he was not missing anything of value.

But Aaron Copland had other and more important reasons for visiting Mexico at this time. Carlos Chávez, a leading Mexican composer and conductor, had invited him many times before, wanting to renew an acquaintance that had begun several years earlier. Aaron was fond of Chávez and wanted to know more about this intense and enthusiastic young man whose life had paralleled Copland's own life in so many ways.

Carlos Chávez was born in 1899. He went to Paris to study in the early nineteen-twenties and subsequently spent several years in New York. As conductor of the Orquesta Sinfonica de México, director of the Conservatoria de México, and a gifted composer, he made many different contributions to the world of music. Like Copland, he had a fervent interest in furthering the cause of modern music and was constantly alert to new developments in the Americas and in Europe. He had already introduced some of Copland's work to Mexican audiences. And in 1938 he wrote a book called *Toward a New Music,* in which he discussed electronic techniques that have just begun to be investigated in the nineteen-sixties.

Aaron decided to make the journey with Victor Kraft, a young photographer who had been looking for an excuse to take pictures of Mexican life. There was a strong element of adventure in the trip, since Mexico was not well known to Americans at that time, and by the vast majority was thought to be a land of dirt, disease, and especially of danger.

Any young traveler who was foolish enough to consider the journey in the first place was subjected to a long list of precautions against the thieves, the heat of the deserts, the cold of the capital, the altitude, and, always and everywhere, the drinking water.

From the very beginning of the trip, with glimpses of little towns along the railway line and of Indians who sometimes clustered in the stations, Aaron was impressed by an atmosphere of antiquity that hung over the country. By comparison Europe seemed young.

In Mexico City, Chávez arranged for cool rooms in a gracious old hotel. The visitors spent the rest of the day of arrival recuperating from the long tiring trip but were at rehearsals for the Copland concert early the next morning. Besides several smaller works, Chávez had scheduled the Piano Variations and *Music for the Theatre.* After listening briefly to Chávez's interpretation of his music, Aaron was aware of a basic understanding that the Mexican conductor had of his work.

His ideas were borne out at the concert, which was a great success with the audience and the press.

As soon as it was over, Aaron and Victor set out for the village of Tlalpam, a charming ancient town not far from Mexico City. Aaron found a house that was in a bad state of repair but had the requisites that both the young men insisted upon: spacious rooms that ensured privacy for each of them, relatively adequate plumbing, and a patio where they might take full advantage of the clear warm autumn days. Also, and perhaps more important, they could see a part of the village life from their own front door.

Although Aaron was impatient to get down to work, the change of air and the heat induced a kind of inertia that was difficult to overcome. Aaron had visited Latin countries before. In Italy he had seen the same kinds of crumbling walls, with great lush tangles of jasmine or honeysuckle climbing over them. He had awakened in the morning to the sound of church bells coming across the cold dry air and listened in the evenings for the sound of the Angelus. Nevertheless, the atmosphere of this ancient place produced the same initial lethargy. It was several days before he could settle down to serious work. In the meantime, he did not regret the lazy afternoons spent watching the lizards scurrying up the sunbaked walls or the soft evening hours when he liked to walk through the village enjoying the aroma of the spicy enchiladas that filled the air.

Soon Aaron was working, or at least trying to work. The routine that had become so much a part of his life was an easy harness in New York, but here it was quite a different matter. At home, almost at will, he could switch on the concentration essential for composition— but where was it now? More and more he gave himself to the slow ancient tempo of the town, exploring its vivid village life and trying to gain insight into the lives of the gentle people.

Work continued on the *Short Symphony,* which he had brought from New York. Slowly Aaron began to feel that he was making progress and before long he was able to turn his attention to the new work that was beginning to occupy his thoughts—the short orchestral work that had been commissioned by the League of Composers for its tenth anniversary celebration.

When Aaron returned to Mexico City, he expected to find the big-city atmosphere that he had missed during his first days there. He wondered if he had been too occupied with thoughts of the concert. But just as before, he felt that in the capital—as all over the rest of Mexico

—a soft mist of time seemed to have fallen. He had the same curious feeling he was to have on subsequent visits, that he had stepped back several centuries.

Carlos Chávez took Aaron on several trips to the surrounding countryside. They visited Cuernavaca, a pleasant resort city famous for its association with the ill-starred Emperor Maximilian and his Empress Carlota. The town was about fifty miles from Mexico City and the route took them over mountains where one spectacular view gave way to another. Chávez was an excellent guide. If there was a particularly interesting fiesta going on anywhere, Chávez knew about it and off they went. During these pleasant hours together, he told Aaron about the origins of Mexico's musical culture. An abiding need of music had persisted until the present day, and everywhere he went, Aaron saw how deeply the daily life of the people was involved with music.

Partly this could be attributed to the climate which permitted so much of the time to be lived out of doors. There was not the sharp division, as in New York, of outdoor, as opposed to indoor, activities. Rather, there was an easy flow of living, back and forth, in and out, that developed the use of music within a wide social pattern. Aaron recalled that he had seen much of this in Italy too—the same intermingling of work, play, and music that is particularly strong in Latin countries.

By now Aaron's Spanish was becoming more fluent with every passing day. Asking directions was no longer an ordeal but a gratifying test of his ability to understand various dialects of the language. Feeling more secure, Aaron began to explore remote parts of the city.

One night when he was lost in an unfamiliar, disreputable section, he suddenly turned a corner that brought him within view of a place where a great many people were having a very good time. It was the brightly lit, smoke-filled rooms of El Salón México, a dance hall that on this Saturday night was bursting with animation and an undercurrent of amorous intention.

Husky young men, many of them looking as though they had just come from the country for a night on the town, stood packed closely together in their fresh white shirts, their thick black hair sleeked with oil and water. Others were dancing *jarabes* with flushed, attractive young women wearing the bright hot pinks, lemon yellows, and greens that appear in Mexican folk art.

The mariachi orchestra was expert, the players fast and strong, and they too seemed to be caught up in the atmosphere of smoldering passion that pervaded the dance hall and spilled out into the street.

Aaron had visited many fiestas and had passed several mariachi orchestras in the streets but never had he heard such staccato rhythms as now, such intensely alive, fast-moving, fast-changing music. Aaron remained at El Salón México until midnight, completely hypnotized, and when he left it was to go home exhausted and drop into bed.

All through the next morning the music of the mariachi orchestra kept repeating itself in Aaron's ears. It was a fascinating combination of instruments that had originally been limited to only strings—violins, guitars, often mandolins, double basses or a small harp. In recent years, Chávez told Aaron, brass instruments, particularly the trumpet, had been added.

Later on, while traveling through different parts of Mexico, Aaron heard the same folk songs in countless variations. He began to realize that there was a great amount of indigenous music that had been neglected by the professional musicians of the country.

He became absorbed in seeking out as much folk music as he could find. He began to mull over the accepted idea of folk music as a rather static form that remained pure or simply disappeared. In reality, this was far from true. As with the folkcrafts, the forms were constantly changing, sometimes being enriched but too often corrupted.

It seemed reasonable to believe that as time went on, certain parts of the old folk songs were forgotten and the improvisation that was added had changed the original form. Undoubtedly the music also changed for the simple reason that one people became impressed with the music of another group and succumbed to the instinctive drive to imitate.

Whatever the actual circumstances were, Aaron was sure that what the world knew as folk and primitive music was not a static form but a constantly changing art that was the fruit of vast numbers of anonymous people. Now that communications and transportation were becoming easier and more rapid, folk music would be in even greater flux.

As time went on, Aaron heard more music by Chávez

and another impressive Mexican composer whose work he admired very much—Silvestre Revueltas. Chávez' music, strong and deliberate, caught the characteristic fatalism of the Indian spirit. It was, Aaron said, ". . . music of per sistence—relentless and uncompromising." It was music that carried with it a strong feeling of the remote past while being highly articulate in the contemporary spirit.

Aaron wrote that just ". . . as Debussy and Ravel reflected the clarity, the delicacy, and wit of the French spirit without recourse to French folklore, so Chávez had learned to write music that caught the spirit of Mexico— its naïve, stolid *Mestizo* soul." He continued to praise Chávez, and in his book *Our New Music* he wrote that ". . . no other composer—not even Béla Bartók or Manuel de Falla—has succeeded so well in using folk material in its pure form while at the same time solving the problem of its complete amalgamation into an art form."

As the weeks in Mexico passed by, the vitality and fascination of El Salón México and its music remained fresh and insistent in Copland's mind. Although he was not aware of it yet, he was beginning to move slowly toward new musical ideas which were to be of great importance in his future development.

He left Mexico in 1933 and began work on the composition which he decided to call simply *El Salón México*. In a version for two pianos, it was first performed on October 11, 1935, at one of the concerts of contemporary music that Aaron organized soon after he resumed his lectures at the New School for Social Research. The orchestral work, first performed in Mexico City in 1937, caught all the lusty, vibrant spirit of the dance hall that Aaron had found so arresting that night several years previously when he had unknowingly stumbled on it. In this work he captured the quality of that night and the music he had heard—lyrically sentimental, often garish or coarse, humorous and ribald, but always intensely robust and alive.

In the program notes that Aaron wrote for the performance of *El Salón México* in Boston, he said that he made no attempt to portray either the Mexico of ancient civilization or the Mexico of modern revolution. The themes were taken directly from two collections of popular Mexican melodies, as fifty years previously Emmanuel Chabrier, the French composer, had composed *España* from the folk music of Spain, or as Béla Bartók had used Hungarian folk tunes.

The influential critic Olin Downes wrote a favorable review but one that was qualified by definite reservations. He found the work a "brilliant adventure in a certain idiom although there is always the danger, where many themes are employed, of a composition that will be patchwork. The danger is competently met by the composer."

"Competently" was a very grudging word to use in reference to *El Salón México,* a work that won an extremely enthusiastic response from audiences all over the world and was to become one of Aaron Copland's most frequently played works. It was his first one to gain the attention of a large international public and its popularity assured it of a regular place on concert programs.

The performance of *El Salón México* in London was a particularly brilliant and successful concert, widely acclaimed by the press and public. This was an important turning point in Copland's career, for it was after this performance that Boosey and Hawkes, prominent English music publishers, gave Aaron a long-term contract that assured each new work of publication soon after its completion.

For the first time, Aaron began to know financial security. It was really from this point on that he never had to face another economic crisis. At the same time, his standing in the international world of music began to strengthen; hardly a conversation anywhere in the world that dealt with American music could ignore the name Copland.

# 15

# *A Vast New Audience*

*El Salón México* was Copland's first work which had a wide audience appeal. He was naturally pleased at the idea that his music was being heard by far greater numbers of people than in the past. But his concern about being heard by large audiences gave many critics the opportunity to speak patronizingly about his "merchandising of folksiness." He was also called a "shrewd investor of little pennies" and much attention was brought to bear on the two Copland styles—one which appealed to a small intelligentsia, the other which had a vast popular appeal and was also very lucrative.

The major broadcasting systems, with a respect for their new audiences which was to disappear in later years, also made the serious composer aware of how drastically the size and nature of his potential audience was chang-

130

ing. They began actively to encourage the writing of new works and put their expert publicity staffs behind these efforts.

In 1936 the Columbia Broadcasting System commissioned six leading American composers to write works that were *specifically* composed for radio. Actually, of course, good music could not be limited in any such way. The main purpose of the commissions was simply to stimulate more interest in radio itself. Besides Aaron Copland, the other composers who received commissions were Howard Hanson, Roy Harris, Walter Piston, Louis Gruenberg, and William Grant Still. One of the requirements was that the work be scored for a large orchestra including three saxophones.

The Columbia Broadcasting System, ever on the lookout to stimulate "audience participation," announced that the composer of its third musical work in the series invited the audience to interpret and name his work. The press release said that temporarily the piece was being called *Music for Radio,* but that "the listener who sends in a permanent title which most successfully tells Mr. Copland what his music is about, will receive an autographed copy of the original score."

Aaron Copland did not care for this blatant kind of promotional publicity but he had little choice but to go along with it. The winning title submitted was *Saga of the Prairie* but the most recent catalogue of Copland's work lists it still as *Music for Radio.*

Now the commissions for *Gebrauchsmusik* began to come in fast. Grace Spofford, the energetic and resourceful music director of the Henry Street Settlement House, suggested that Aaron write a work for young people which would be produced by the music school of the settlement house. Several ambitious productions, including Kurt Weill's *Der Jasager* (The Man Who Always Said Yes) and Paul Hindemith's *Wir Bauen Eine Stat* (Let's Build a City), had already been successful. These were good examples of European *Gebrauchsmusik* but Miss Spofford wanted to find a version that would reflect American life.

Copland began composing the score for this work in January 1936, the same year that he finished the final orchestration of *El Salón México*. In June he left again for Tlaxcala, Mexico, where the writer Edwin Denby, who was to do the libretto, joined him. Toward the end of the year Copland finished the work, which was called *The Second Hurricane*—perhaps one of the first examples of American *Gebrauchsmusik* in play-opera form.

The story concerns an aviator who is doing rescue work in a flooded area that has been devastated by a hurricane. He finds the volunteer helpers he needs in a local school. But while he is flying the children to the danger area, a sudden warning tells of the approach of a second hurricane.

Because of engine trouble, the aviator is forced to land on a hill where he leaves the children while he flies elsewhere to get his engine repaired. As soon as he leaves the scene, disorder reigns because none of the children is willing to take orders or to cooperate with each other. It is only when the second hurricane strikes and they are placed in immediate danger that they become aware of the need to work together.

Soon the children are saved and brought to a place where they can aid the flood victims. They realize that by working cooperatively they can achieve quick, successful results.

*The Second Hurricane* was put into production by two talented men of the theater, Lehman Engel, the conductor, and Orson Welles, who acted as director. Virgil Thomson called the music "vigorous and noble," the libretto, "fresh and permeated with great sweetness." Much of the work's success can be attributed to Copland's understanding of the capacities and level of skill which young people of high school age possess. He had had a good chance to observe such young people during the years from 1935 to 1939 when he taught at the Settlement House, and now he put this knowledge to good use.

Copland had come a long way from the Piano Variations and there were criticisms about his descending to popular taste. But during these years he was firmly decided upon the direction in which to go. When Alexander Richter, then director of music for the New York High School of Music and Art, attended the performance of *The Second Hurricane* he was so impressed that he commissioned Copland to write a new work for the high school orchestra. He believed this was an area of music that had been neglected, and he hoped to stimulate interest in this field by a campaign that he called "American Music for American Youth." Richter thought it would be an excellent idea if Aaron Copland "sounded the opening gun."

He suggested that the work be limited to one movement of perhaps five or ten minutes' duration and that it be in the form of an overture or rhapsody. The result of this commission was *Outdoor Overture,* which is a perennial favorite of high school orchestras.

As the nineteen-thirties closed, Copland received a commission which was a forerunner of the many new assignments for theater and film music that the years ahead were to bring. This was the commission to write the score for *The City,* a documentary film which was shown at the 1939–40 New York World's Fair. The film had been made by a group of architects who wanted to propagandize the value of planned urban communities. The excellent photography and clever editing sharply contrasted grim slum areas with the clean open character of an intelligently planned urban area.

It was an almost made-to-order opportunity for Copland to make good use of his special ability to evoke the various aspects of a huge city and also the contemplative melancholy that such cities often arouse in their inhabitants. In this work Copland achieves the effect by the use of a trumpet and English horn which carry the dialogue simply but movingly against a background of strings. Hearing this music, one recalls Wilfred Meller's perceptive comments about the general character of Copland's talent. "Other men have written greater music in the twentieth century," he wrote, "but nowhere do we find so central and completely musical an expression of the largely unconscious reaction of sensitive people to an industrial environment. The contours of his music are sharp and incisive and uncompromising as a machine but they are also full of human pity and tenderness."

Almost immediately this accomplishment bore fruit that was to open up great new possibilities for Copland's creative energies.

In 1938 Aaron returned to a Europe that was in a bad state of war jitters. The reason for the trip was the European premiere, in London, of *El Salón México*. At the concert, sponsored by the International Society for Contemporary Music, Copland met the brilliant young English composer Benjamin Britten, then only twenty-four years old.

Just a few days before the concert Copland heard his first Britten piece, *Variations on a Theme of Frank Bridge*, and was delighted with the "technical adroitness and wizardry" of this early work.

After the performance of *El Salón México*, Britten invited Aaron to spend a weekend with him at his home in a small village in Suffolk, East Anglia.

Britten lived in a charming reconverted windmill that had wonderful views of the surrounding fields and thatch-roofed houses that dotted the countryside. Above, huge masses of white clouds hung majestically in a sky that reminded Copland of the great English landscape paintings that he had just seen in London's National Gallery. The extraordinary feeling of space made him recall his own urban loft studio set among the skyscrapers of New York.

Britten took Copland and some other friends to visit the shingles, a rather bleak English beach. Aaron had never been a sun worshiper and when everyone took off as much clothing as decency permitted, he made the gesture of taking off a heavy sweater.

The English were delighted, as always, by the appearance of a day of uninterrupted sunlight and were determined to take advantage of it. As pale, white skins turned a dangerous pink, Aaron walked along the shore exploring the coastline that had such an austere quality compared to the American beaches.

Later on, after tea, Aaron showed Britten the proofs of *The Second Hurricane,* which he had with him. "It didn't take much persuasion," he wrote, "to get me to play it from start to finish, singing all the parts of the principals and chorus in the usual composer fashion."

Britten seemed pleased by the work and Copland sometimes wondered afterward if the young composer's preoccupation with young voices might be partly an offshoot of his pleasure in *The Second Hurricane.*

Britten, in turn, played his recently completed Piano Concerto No. 1. At once Copland was struck by the obvious flair for idiomatic piano writing in the concerto "but had some reservations as to the substance of the musical materials." There was much to talk about—modern music, the men of music, the history of music. Several months later when Britten came to the United States to live for a time, Aaron and the British composer continued the friendship that began so auspiciously in England.

On Copland's next visit to London he was oppressed by the ominous mood in the city. The possibility of another world war, and how quickly it might come, were constant subjects of conversation. Those who saw it as imminent were right, of course. Within a year, children would be playing in the newly dug trenches of Hyde Park, frightening each other with their gas masks. People began to hoard food and were not allowed to forget the crisis by the signs that read "Keep Calm—and Dig." The growing sense of urgency and the fear of the future were quickly caught by American travelers who cut short their European trips and made plans to return home. They would not be visiting Europe again for several years.

# 16

## Tanglewood

Copland has never been completely at ease in the role of teacher. Even at the Henry Street Settlement House during the year 1936–37 he arranged to have his students come to his studio instead of his going to the school. It was Koussevitzky who strongly urged Copland to resume the teaching position again. After becoming director of the Berkshire Symphonic Festival at Tanglewood, Koussevitzky knew that the music center could flourish only if it had the best creative talent there to guide it. He asked Copland to come.

The first festival took place in the summer of 1934 in the old horse-show ring at the Hanna Farm in Stockbridge in the heart of the rolling, verdant hills of the Berkshire Mountains of Massachusetts. It was a makeshift affair that included all the inconveniences usually associated with outdoor musical enjoyment.

138

The benches were hard, the air was damp and cold, the ground was bumpy and wet. Someone reported that "the strings on the violins snapped like popcorn." It was not an auspicious beginning but each succeeding year brought improvements that were to make the Berkshire Festival and its Music Center among the most vital and important of their kind in the country.

As the festival began to attract more people, larger facilities soon became necessary. With great generosity, Mrs. Gorham Brooks and her aunt, Miss Mary Aspinwall Tappan, offered to make a gift of their estate Tanglewood to the Boston Symphony Orchestra.

The name was taken from Nathaniel Hawthorne's *Tanglewood Tales for Girls and Boys,* a collection of stories written while he was living in a small red cottage on the grounds. Hawthorne loved the rocks, streams, and deep woods, particularly those woods that in the summer became a lush, green tangle of growing things.

Koussevitzky gave a vast amount of his time and energy to Tanglewood and was responsible for the creation in 1940, of the Berkshire Music Center, partly financed by the Rockefeller Foundation. In 1941 a Theater-Concert Hall, designed by Eero Saarinen, the Finnish architect, was built and later the same year, a new hall intended especially for chamber music. The main building on the estate is used for administrative offices, studios, and a library. After all the ambitious construction, two hundred acres of fields, woods, and lawns still remain.

During the Music Center's first season there were

over three hundred carefully selected students who were chosen from auditions in various cities by Koussevitzky and his staff. Most of them were under thirty years of age.

Koussevitzky asked Aaron to assume the heavy responsibilities of both assistant director and head of the Composition Department. Among the many distinguished guest teachers who came to teach in this department in the following years were Darius Milhaud and Paul Hindemith.

In addition to his regular teaching, Copland was also active on the Tanglewood Forum, where he acted as moderator. A variety of subjects connected with the world of music were discussed by a panel of informal speakers. Each one was allotted ten minutes. Some of the topics that aroused heated discussions in the nineteen-forties were nationalism in American music, the future of the opera in America, and whether the government should help the arts.

It was also Copland's responsibility to arrange the Sunday night concerts of students' works drawn from both the composition and instrumental departments.

The American prodigy Leonard Bernstein (later to become director of the New York Philharmonic Orchestra) did not formally study composition with Copland but he often submitted his work for an opinion. He said he profited a great deal from their conversations. Sometimes Aaron would say, "This is lousy, and this sounds like Scriabin . . . ," continuing with the candor that only fond friendship permits, ". . . but go home and write some more." It was a very informal kind of teaching but

Copland's influence was and still is of great importance in Bernstein's work.

For the young composer working at Tanglewood, the conditions are unique. The best works written generally have a good chance of being played during the summer course. The course itself is short, intensive, and concentrated. The pace is so accelerated that it would be difficult to sustain the creative tension for a much longer period.

Often after a grueling discussion of difficult technical matters the conversation would turn to a more abstract consideration of the nature of creativity. Copland summed up some of his thoughts on this subject in his book *Music and Imagination*. To the questions "Why is it so important . . . that I compose music? What makes it seem so absolutely necessary, so that every daily activity, by comparison, is of lesser significance? And why is the creative impulse never satisfied; why must one always begin anew?" he answered that, as far as the first question was concerned, the answer was always the same —"self-expression; the basic need to make evident one's deepest feeling about life." In answer to the other questions—the unceasing need to begin again—he wrote: "The reason for the compulsion to renewed creativity . . . is that each added work brings with it an element of self-discovery. I must create in order to know myself and since self-knowledge is a never-ending search, each new work is only a part answer to the question, 'Who am I?' "

It was inevitable that the work of many of these young composers should reveal Copland's influence. It is safe to guess that during the twenty-five years that he served at Tanglewood, more students came within the range of his influence than that of any other major American composer. He has been called the dean and spiritual father of more than one generation of American composers.

And yet the young people who worked with him never formed the kind of coterie that gathers around so many great creative people, faithfully imitating the aesthetic ideals of their teachers. Copland was unique in always being able to view his students' work with a pure objectivity that was relatively free of bias. He never suggested a Coplandesque solution for a problem that could be solved only within the context which the student had created. In later years many of these students recalled "his wit . . . reasoned judgment, an absolute lack of façade, self-importance, or bigotry of any kind."

After Koussevitzky's death in 1951, Charles Munch became director of the Boston Symphony Orchestra and took over the work at Tanglewood. Munch found that he had as much responsibility as he wanted with the Boston Symphony and turned the chairmanship of the faculty over to Copland.

Many years later Aaron Copland wrote about the "responsibilities of music citizenship." He said that "the music community, like any other, imposes duties on its citizens, and it has always been important to me to assume my fair share of them." It would be difficult to dispute the fact that Aaron Copland has assumed more than a "fair share" of those duties—and has performed them with excellence.

# 17

## Assignments in Hollywood

In 1937 Hollywood Boulevard did not yet have the penny-arcade atmosphere that was to surprise and disappoint so many visitors in later years. There were smart shops and some excellent restaurants of the sort that display autographed caricatures of their more famous patrons. If the food was good, it was often because it had been prepared by a recently arrived refugee from Berlin or Vienna, one who knew precisely what went into the preparation of a really good apple strudel or Wiener schnitzel à la Holstein.

These refugees were then pouring into the country in greater numbers every year. In their dark clothes cut in the European manner, they often looked strangely out of place in the bright sunshine and palm tree landscape of southern California.

143

The news had quickly spread in the East that several European artists of international prominence had chosen Hollywood as their home in exile. After decades of damp continental winters, the California climate was a delight to them—as was the year-round abundance of fresh fruits and vegetables.

Among the distinguished artists who went to Los Angeles were the famous German anti-Fascist writer Thomas Mann and Aldous Huxley, an Englishman who was among the first writers to describe his experiences with the newly discovered drug LSD. In January these men were able to stroll the beaches together, talking of Shakespeare and music.

The writer Christopher Isherwood was soon to follow, making his permanent home in Santa Monica. Before long, Arnold Schönberg would be teaching music at the University of California at Los Angeles. And perched high in the Hollywood Hills was a charming Spanish-style house where Igor Stravinsky began to stoke anew those creative fires that burned brightly in any country or climate.

Aaron Copland had wanted to see Hollywood for a long time. And he wanted to write more film scores. The level of most film music was abysmally low, but occasionally an enlightened director or producer insisted upon hiring a talented composer instead of the usual hack for a film of special importance. The salaries paid to the men working in films were astronomical and now, in the lean year of 1937, it seemed like a good time to explore the possibilities of more film work.

Aaron looked up old friends, settled down in a small hotel near Sunset Boulevard and read *Variety*. So many writers and composers had come west looking for work during these years that they had become a glut on the market. Even then, as Aaron discovered, Hollywood felt most tenderly toward those whom it had summoned from a distance—and the greater the distance, the more tender the feelings.

After several weeks of fruitless searching for work, Aaron decided to return to New York, where a sudden burst of new assignments kept him busy. In less than two years, Hollywood would be calling.

In 1938 John Steinbeck's famous novel *Of Mice and Men* was assigned to the distinguished film director Lewis Milestone. He intended to do everything possible to make the book into a great film. He chose the cast and crew after much deliberation, and when the actual shooting began and the rushes started to arrive every day, he felt sure that a film of great beauty and significance was in the making. He was determined that the score should have the same high quality as the rest of the film. One night, as he watched *The City* at the home of a friend, he knew that he had his man.

The Music Corporation of America was the agency that negotiated all of Copland's contracts and obtained new assignments. They wired their office in New York that the terms were generous and should be accepted. Before agreeing, however, Aaron bought a copy of the famous book and settled down to reread Steinbeck's absorbing tale of two itinerant farm workers—one gentle and wise, the other a sympathetic but mentally deficient giant of a man—who become involved in a tragedy on one of the great wheat farms of northern California.

Aaron had read the book when it was first published but he wanted to refresh his memory and make absolutely sure that it was a work which would be able to arouse his own creative powers. The second reading convinced him that it was, and he instructed the agency's New York office to wire acceptance. Within twenty-four hours he was packing for the journey west.

Watching the film in the studio projection room, Aaron knew that this was a work which was particularly well suited to his own talents. *Of Mice and Men* was not an ordinary film. Lon Chaney, Jr., Betty Field, and Burgess Meredith were distinguished actors who gave excellent performances. Visually the film was very exciting. Nothing of the artificial studio set obtruded because the cameraman had insisted upon shooting on location as much as possible. A powerful sense of drama had been achieved, and, even before the film was over, certain musical ideas suggested themselves to Aaron. That night before going to sleep he made notations on the backs of envelopes and looked forward to the next morning when he could return to the studio.

He was deeply moved by the film and this, as he emphasized in later years, was a touchstone of greatest importance for the composer of film music. He wrote in *Our New Music:*

Where there is not true expressive purpose, anything goes; in fact, everything goes, and it all goes into the same piece. The so-called Hollywood orchestration is a composite of all the known tricks in the orchestrator's bag . . . it is rare to hear a score that strikes one as touching because of the fact that the composer himself was moved by the action of the film.

Aaron plunged into work. It was as if the enthusiasm that he had felt on first seeing the film was enough to ignite his creativity anew each day.

Usually he slept until eleven or twelve o'clock. Lying in bed, he would listen for the familiar sounds of the New York traffic outside his window and then realize with a sudden burst of pleasure that he was in California. He would go to the window and draw the curtains to let in that miraculous winter warmth and sunlight that was a never-ending delight. The broad boulevards in 1939 were relatively free of traffic. In midwinter the lawns were green and well cared for, bright with roses and banks of pink and white vine geraniums. Before long the acacias with their great masses of golden yellow flowers would be in bloom. Aaron enjoyed every minute of all this— as long as he knew that his studio in New York was waiting for him.

His office, with its large desk and view of a huge sound stage, was not inspiring. Aaron would chat with his secretary, inwardly amused that the studio officials thought he needed such an assistant, glance over the mail, and then leave as quickly as possible for a long lunch.

At one thirty the studio commissary was a busy place, bustling with activity and noisy and animated with intense and often highly spirited conversations.

Besides the actors, there were the craftsmen, dancers in costume, designers, art directors, and the usual hordes of press men with their guests. In all the studio commissaries there are unofficial tables that are reserved primarily for writers, directors, or other workers with special creative interests. Not limiting himself to any one group, Aaron enjoyed the conversations of many different people.

Almost reluctantly, he returned to his office around three o'clock, when his workday began. At five thirty, as in many other places of business, most of the people would leave for home. The studio streets would fill as secretaries, technicians, wardrobe mistresses, and workers in many other crafts left for home. But it was not uncommon for work to continue on one or more of the sound stages where actual filming was in progress. The film editing and sound departments often worked late as well, but by ten or eleven the studio was generally deserted except for the night watchmen and the uniformed police at the gates.

For Copland this was the best time, perhaps the only time, when he could crowd out the distractions of California and the studio itself and get down to the business in hand.

By eleven o'clock the studio seemed far removed from the glittering city around it. The sound stages, with their high gray windowless walls, made the scene look almost medieval. Many of the studio streets were deep in shadow except for the small lights at corners. It was his lonely work late during the night among the forbidding-looking sound stages that gave Aaron the highly individual and unusual impression that he carries of Hollywood as a dark, medieval place.

Around midnight or one o'clock he would wearily get his things together, nod cheerfully to the drowsy gateman fighting sleep in his gatehouse, and walk to his car. Too exhilarated to return home at once, Aaron would often stop to eat at Barney's Beanery, a small restaurant at the foot of the Hollywood Hills where film people often gathered for hamburgers or a bowl of chili.

Aaron had to learn quickly certain arts essential to the composer of music for films. He was given a movie-ola, a small machine which makes it possible for one to be his own movie operator. With this device he could see the picture as often as he wished while he worked and re-worked a musical idea. He learned the great importance of synchronization, that is, the need for the sound track to work simultaneously with the exact sections of the film for which it is intended. And he learned calmly to meet the day of recording, when he must hear his music for the first time as the film itself is shown.

The rerecording sessions in the dubbing room—where the music is combined with the other sound tracks—Copland called "a kind of composer's purgatory." This is often a painful time, for it is then that the composer hears much of his music muffled as the various characters speak. Aaron said that this is the place "that calls out all a composer's self-control; it is a moment for philosophy."

Many years of experience in writing music for the ballet and theater had given Aaron the background essential for his work as a film composer. In addition, he had the particular type of imagination and insight which such work demands of a composer. The essential thing is the ability to create a mood, to visualize an event and translate it into orchestral terms in much the same way that Hector Berlioz and Franz Liszt created a theatrical mood in their work.

It has been said that one of the difficulties of composing for the films is the necessity of working within the confines of the stopwatch. For it is the stopwatch, measuring the exact duration of scenes, which dictates precisely how long various sections of the music must be. Aaron Copland did not feel restricted by any such limitations. It was, he said, normal procedure for a composer to shorten or lengthen sections of the composition on which he was working.

The men in the music department were not optimistic about the immediate future of film music. In Hollywood, the usual procedure was for the producer to spend a vast amount of time and money in getting the right story, director, and actors, shoot the best film he could, and then turn it over to a musical hack to write the music. After months or even years spent on the actual shooting of a film, composers were generally asked to produce the score in a matter of a few weeks. The usual time allotted for composition is two weeks, but Copland insisted upon six for writing the score for *Of Mice and Men.*

He frequently heard musicians and composers in Hollywood complain that as far as most producers were concerned, the music department and its composers were only "accessories after the fact." Perhaps this attitude toward film music had its origins in the days of the silent films. When these first appeared, there was a great demand for musicians of every type. Amateurism flourished and it is probably safe to estimate that among the thousands of solo or ensemble players who worked in the theaters very few were professional musicians.

As the years went on, film music continued to be regarded as a necessary but relatively unimportant adjunct. However, there were several notable exceptions to this in Europe where, as early as 1928, Darius Milhaud had written an impressive score for the silent film called *Actualités,* first performed at the Music Festival in Baden-Baden, Germany.

In Hollywood, meanwhile, American composers continued to have a low place in the film hierarchy. Their work continued to be mainly a rehash of Brahms, Tchaikovsky, and Wagner. Among the few exceptions that were particularly admired by Copland were Werner Jannsen's score for *The General Died at Dawn* and Ernest Toch's *Ibbetson.*

The score for *Of Mice and Men* was a great success. Copland's interpretation, in purely musical terms, of the emotional conflicts of the characters is incisive and masterful. One typical example is the scene in which Curly, the brutal but cowardly foreman, attacks Lenny, the mentally retarded giant. The blows which Curley hammers home are stylized in a series of "sharp staccato brass chords which are harmonically unrelated, dancing at random over the score. These finally coalesce into an enormous grinding discord" when Lenny, suddenly deciding to retaliate, crushes Curly's hand.

Here Copland has taken a highly dramatic situation and heightened it even further by exciting appropriate music. Throughout the entire score, whether he is expressing the boredom and exasperation of the farmer's daughter, or Lenny's sloppy guzzling of food, Copland's music intensifies the dramatic image on the screen. Where power and full dramatic force are required, the music functions perfectly to underscore the action while still not diverting attention to itself. "After all," Aaron wrote, "film music makes sense only if it helps the film; no matter how good, distinguished, or successful, the music must be secondary in importance to the story being told on the screen."

It is Aaron Copland's fine, instinctive sense of restraint that elevates his film work far above that of most other composers who have worked in this medium. Invariably, the musical stylization develops naturally from what he *feels* about the dramatic work and it is the genuineness of that original emotion that determines the course of the music.

Before long, the prominent producer Sol Lesser offered Copland an assignment that became an important contribution to one of the most sensitive and beautiful films ever made in Hollywood, *Our Town*. This was based on

Thornton Wilder's successful play, which deals with small-town life in a New England village called Grover's Corners.

The action of the film runs from 1901 to 1913 and concerns the lives of two families in neighboring households. George and Emily play with each other as children, fall in love in adolescence, and marry as soon as they graduate from high school.

The characters are as familiar as the boy and girl next door. They move in an exact temporal setting and yet throughout the film we are made to feel aware of infinity and a haunting sense of timelessness. It is a story that calls for music of enormous sensitivity and poignancy—words that in fact epitomize Copland's unforgettable score.

Thornton Wilder wrote *Our Town* while at the MacDowell Colony. Perhaps the fact that Aaron had worked there too and was familiar with the life of the countryside —with its serene, unhurried pace—was partly responsible for his masterful musical evocation of the precise mood that Wilder had achieved with words.

In any event, the film *Our Town* was received with the high praise and acclaim that had been given *Of Mice and Men*. In the years that followed its appearance, Copland was offered many film assignments but carefully chose only those that excited his deepest interest.

Samuel Goldwyn's *The North Star,* produced in 1943, was the story of Russian peasant resistance during World War II. The film was poorly directed and is the least successful of all of Copland's film work.

One of his best-known film scores was that which he wrote for John Steinbeck's *The Red Pony,* produced in 1948. It was an excellent film that captured the fresh beauty of outdoor life on a ranch in the Far West.

When Efrem Kurtz, the new director of the Houston Symphony, asked Copland to write a work especially for his first concert, Aaron adapted a suite from *The Red Pony* and this became one of his most popular works. He calls it a "children's suite because much of the music is intended to reflect a child's world." Herbert Roussel, critic of the Houston *Post,* summed up the response of the public when he called the suite "clear, joyous, ingenious, and irresistibly spirited music . . . by turns tender, and bombastic in a light whimsical manner, well studded with humorous dissonance, it made everybody feel good."

It was *The Heiress,* a film based on Henry James's novel *Washington Square,* that won Aaron Copland the Academy Award for the best film score of the year 1948. With Olivia de Haviland in the starring role, the film achieved a powerfully sustained drama of Victorian New York.

During these years of assignments in Hollywood, Copland had much time to dwell on the nature of film music and its total effect on film audiences. He reasoned that since a large part of the music heard by the American public is heard in the film theater, his music should be of as high a level as any other music.

"Why shouldn't the music critic cover the important film premieres?" he asked. It seemed certain that producers and directors who knew that their pictures would be reviewed consistently and carefully by important music critics would soon pay more attention to the quality of the film scores they commissioned. By bringing this music to a higher level, they would automatically contribute to the musical education and pleasure of the entire theater-going public.

This was an excellent idea but one which has not been realized. Without knowing it, Copland had been working in Hollywood during one of its most fertile periods. In the nineteen-fifties and sixties the number of films produced there declined rapidly as a large part of studio operations was taken over by the burgeoning television industry. The hard pressed producers of full-length films were even less disposed to concern themselves with the quality of the scores of their pictures. Copland was to return to Hollywood many times in the coming years but not to create music. He came to record, to speak, and more and more frequently, to conduct.

# 18

## Great Achievements in the Theater

Aaron Copland had been hearing more and more about the talented young choreographer Agnes de Mille. She had also been hearing about Aaron Copland, and when an important new assignment came up, she asked her agent to arrange a meeting between them. As she said later, the agent had promised her "the best composer."

Agnes de Mille was known for her strong will and peppery personality. In fact, a mutual friend had described her as a rather plump, fresh-looking young woman with the soul of an infantry sergeant.

It was a very informal meeting, with her conductor, Franz Allers, sitting on the only chair that the studio contained, Agnes de Mille seated on the piano bench, and

156

Aaron Copland lying on her bed propped up by a mound of pillows.

Miss de Mille told Copland the gist of the scenario. It was the story of a young cowgirl who acts and dresses like a man. It is her way of staying as close as possible to the head cowboy with whom she is in love. But the only thing that she accomplishes is the annoyance of the cowhands and mockery from most of the women. Finally, she wins her man by putting on a skirt.

"To sum it up," Miss de Mille concluded in her abrupt, salty manner, "it isn't Hamlet but it can have what Martha Graham calls 'an aura of race memory.' "

They all laughed and while Miss de Mille and Allers chatted about other details of the work, Aaron mulled over the idea of the scenario. At first it seemed a bit presumptuous of the Ballet Russe de Monte Carlo, which had commissioned the work, to suppose that they could handle a theme with such a decided American flavor. Perhaps, Copland reasoned to himself, something else might be more appropriate. "Couldn't we do a ballet about Ellis Island?" he asked after a while. Ellis Island was the immigration center for millions who arrived from Europe around the turn of the century. "That I would love to compose," Aaron said enthusiastically.

Miss de Mille's answer would not have surprised other people who had worked with her but Aaron was somewhat taken aback when she raised her voice and sharply said, "You can go to hell!"

Franz Allers, who had been listening carefully, jumped to his feet, afraid that the gentle Copland would not take well to Miss de Mille's fiery outspokenness. "What is happening?" he asked, knowing full well exactly what was happening.

Agnes let just the suggestion of a smile form on her lips. "Mr. Copland and I have just reached a basic understanding." Then turning to him, she said, "You'll get the scenario by post tomorrow. If you like it all, come to tea."

By noon of the next day, Copland was on the phone. "Put the kettle on!" he said.

He arrived at a time that would have been more suitable for lunch than tea, but he couldn't stem his growing delight with the project. Miss de Mille and Aaron spent the rest of the afternoon blocking out the ballet, minute by minute. The final version of the choreography was changed only slightly from that first rough draft.

By early morning, Agnes, having spent the night brooding over the plan she had given to Aaron, was on the telephone again. "You'd better just forget all about the twilight scene," she said with resignation. "I keep forgetting that I simply cannot choreograph lyrically."

"Too bad," Aaron replied. "I've composed it already." Agnes, by now quite bewildered and astonished at Aaron's extraordinary speed, dashed over to his studio. He played the piece for her and she was delighted with it. She realized that she had put something in motion that had now begun to take on a definite life of its own. The twilight scene was *in*.

But there were the usual problems that develop in any collaboration and Agnes de Mille, whose reputation was to be made by *Rodeo,* was still worried about a "possible divergence of style."

Once again Aaron's inner calm smoothed the way. He put a "masterful hand" on her arm and went ahead with the work as they had first conceived it. From time to time Agnes would press him to alter the course. Then Aaron would smile reassuringly and say, "Now Agnes . . . ," and go blithely on his way. He was absolutely convinced that he was on the right track and at this point Miss de Mille had to have faith in his concept.

*Rodeo* was one of the great successes of the season and became a well-loved part of the Ballet Russe de Monte Carlo's repertoire. All the familiar adjectives from "touching" to "enchanting" were made good use of by the critics who were as enthusiastic as the audience itself. *Rodeo* is composed of four dance episodes called "Buckaroo Holiday," "Corral Nocturne," "Saturday Night Waltz," and the "Hoe-Down." The music became a perennial favorite with the American public.

But *Rodeo* was not Copland's first ballet with a western setting. It was preceded by an equally famous theater work entitled *Billy the Kid,* which was produced by the Ballet Caravan in 1938. Billy was not a fictional character; he had been a colorful figure of actual wild West history. The saga of his loves, his lawlessness, and finally his death were exactly the basic elements needed at a time when the American ballet was seeking to create new works with a real American flavor. Copland later arranged a concert suite from this ballet.

It was 1942, the first year of America's participation in World War II. As the holocaust went on, people began to have a greater interest in the arts—but with an emphasis that was different from that of the previous decade. Destruction was sweeping across many parts of the world and people who were now confronted with news of death and violence whenever they read a newspaper or turned on the radio began to search for some deeper meaning in life. They hoped to find that meaning in art forms such as the theater, literature, and music.

Stephen Spender, the English poet, wrote in *World Within World* that during this period

> . . . audiences at the midday concerts of the National Gallery [in London], or at the recitals of music and ballet in provincial towns and at factories, sat with rapt attention as though they were listening for some message from the artist who, though perhaps he lived in other times, was close to the same realities as themselves—and the pressing need to affirm and find joy within them.

By 1942 the war had begun to dominate most aspects of American life. Along with other workers everywhere, artists wanted to serve their country. In the interests of national morale, Andre Kostelanetz, the symphony conductor, commissioned Aaron Copland and several other composers to write musical portraits of great Americans.

Because Copland had always been fascinated by the work of Walt Whitman, this seemed like the perfect moment to write a work based on this poet's grand vision of life. But Jerome Kern, one of the other composers who had received a commission, had chosen Mark Twain and Kostelanetz did not want to have two literary men in the series.

Copland's next choice was Abraham Lincoln. But Virgil Thomson, who had chosen New York's Mayor Fiorello H. La Guardia as his subject, suggested that it would be difficult for any composer to put into purely musical terms the exalted stature of Abraham Lincoln. Copland listened carefully to Thomson's intelligent comments and decided that the music should be integrated with Lincoln's own words. It was an act of humility, for by doing this Copland deliberately limited the prestige which, as a pure work of music, it might have had. His aim was to suggest "something of the mysterious sense of fatality that surrounds Lincoln's personality as well as something of his gentleness and simplicity of spirit."

He immediately began a study of Lincoln's letters and speeches, many of which were as meaningful and timely in 1942 as they had been in 1862.

He began the work in February 1942 and finished the orchestration by May. Brief quotations from two songs of the period—Stephen Foster's "Camptown Races" and the folk song "Springfield Mountain"—contribute a quality of nostalgia to the work.

*A Lincoln Portrait* was first performed by the Cincinnati Symphony and shortly afterward was broadcast on the symphony's Sunday concert hour. Aaron gave a brief introduction and Carl Sandburg read the text. It is a moving tribute to one of the nation's greatest men and has become a familiar part of Lincoln's Birthday celebrations.

During these years a great deal was written about the "two Coplands." For some unknown reason, the public, and many critics as well, become acutely uneasy if an artist's newest work does not share certain basic features of his earlier output. Experimentation in many widely divergent forms or styles can be a dangerous path for the artist to take and few have survived its pitfalls. Igor Stravinsky and Pablo Picasso are two of the most famous, but Stravinsky has often come under fire for his variety of styles.

Copland insists that there has never been a divergence in his style. He flatly remarks: "As I see it, music that is born complex is not inherently better or worse than music that is born simple." But this statement has never satisfied those people who want things put into a clear and rigid pattern. To such people it was very disturbing that, for example, the Piano Variations had elements of dissonance and lacked tunes that they could recognize or associate with literary images, while other works such as *Rodeo* filled their minds with visions of western sunlight and vigorous outdoor life.

One day in 1943 Mrs. Elizabeth Sprague Coolidge, a generous patron of the arts, called Martha Graham and said: "I think the time has arrived when you should have some music written especially for you." Miss Graham's reputation as the country's leading choreographer of modern dance was growing but financial rewards were slow to come. She welcomed the kind offer and was not surprised when Mrs. Coolidge—who was very fond of Copland's work—suggested him as the first composer to be considered.

Martha Graham was delighted with the idea because she had followed Copland's music with increasing interest since she first heard the Piano Variations. The basic idea of the dance which she proposed to him could be traced to her childhood memories of her ninety-six-year old grandmother who had spent most of her life on a beautiful old farm in Pennsylvania. Martha Graham still cherished the handmade quilts and silver that had been handed down to her, and her thoughts often returned to the vigorous outdoor life that her forebears had lived.

The work was first performed on October 30, 1944, in the new Coolidge Auditorium in the Library of Congress at Washington, D.C., in a special performance honoring the eightieth birthday of Mrs. Coolidge. Martha Graham still vividly recalls the excitement of the opening night heightened still further by the precautions that are always taken in the Library of Congress. Everything that she had brought—her ironing board and iron, her Fortuny dress carefully tied and wrapped—all had to be inspected to make sure that a bomb was not concealed somewhere.

Copland, who had gone to Mexico for the summer, hurried back to be present for the opening night. Soon after he arrived he called Martha at her hotel and asked, "Have you found a title yet?"—for she had still been searching for one when he left.

"Yes," she answered immediately, "a beautiful title—from a poem by Hart Crane. I'm calling the ballet *Appalachian Spring*."

That was the first that Aaron Copland knew about the dance having anything to do with a particular season.

And it has amused him during the years that have passed, when so many people came to him after a performance to exclaim, "Oh, Mr. Copland, I can just *hear* spring in your music!"

At once, the special Copland quality of a simple austerity sets the mood of *Appalachian Spring* and we find ourselves in some past time of pastoral beauty and life lived in harmony with the rhythms of nature. The harmonic treatment of the work is based chiefly on open fourths and fifths, by now a Copland signature. Soon we are involved in a dance-drama far removed in time from the life of modern urban America.

Although the work has the flavor of Shaker dances, songs, and hymns, Copland used only one source directly —the Shaker hymn called "Simple Gifts," which he discovered in Edward D. Andrews' collection of *Shaker Folklore* entitled "The Gift to Be Simple." It conveys the spirit of this small religious sect which was joyous in spite of the ascetic, communal form of life led by its members.

### SIMPLE GIFTS

'Tis the gift to be simple,
'Tis the gift to be free,
'Tis the gift to come down
Where we ought to be,
And when we find ourselves
In the place just right,
'Twill be in the valley of
Love and Delight

The program notes, written by Martha Graham, said that "spring was celebrated by a man and a woman building a house with joy and love and prayer; by a revivalist and his followers in their shouts of exultation; by a pioneering woman with her dreams of the promised land."

In a symbolic sense that woman was Martha Graham, one of the greatest pioneers in the field of modern dance. Copland attributes much of the character of the music itself to his own feeling about Martha Graham as an individual. Her feeling for tragedy, her ascetic nature were often in his thoughts as he wrote *Appalachian Spring*. Later he said: "Two things were in my mind as I worked on this commission; my own knowledge of rural America in the nineteenth century and my knowledge of Martha Graham. I put her personality to music."

The choreographer has her own very firm ideas about the nature of creation and collaboration. "One doesn't make anything happen, one doesn't direct," she said. "You select an artist, someone you believe in, such as Aaron Copland. And then you let it ride—high, wide, and handsome." After the performance, Martha Graham said that she felt that the work   the combined efforts of her own choreography, Copland's music, and Isamu Noguchi's set designs—would be a work that would live. In the music especially she saw what she calls "Copland's absolute purity."

The critics were enthusiastic too, immediately aware that a work of high achievement had taken place. A review in *Modern Music* stated: "Copland's *Appalachian Spring* was the real exhilaration of the evening. Here were the tart herbs of plain American speech, the pasture, without the flowers of elocution . . . the clean rhythms . . . the irony and homespun tenderness that, in a fine peroration, reached a sustained exaltation."

Virgil Thomson wrote: "The style is pastoral, the tone, as is appropriate to the pastoral style, blithe and beatific. The instrumentation is plain, clean-colored, deeply imaginative. It is designed not only to express the moods of the story but to amplify the characteristics of the dramatis personnae." He concluded by referring to ". . . those special Copland moments when the whole musical texture reaches an ultimate of thinness and translucency," perhaps some of the most truly descriptive words that have ever been written about Copland.

The work was originally scored for only thirteen instruments. But for the concert adaptation Copland expanded the instrumental forces to the standard symphonic dimensions. Koussevitzky's famous recording did much to spread the popularity of this work. He was particularly adept at the development of subtle but rich orchestral sonority. The composition provided an opportunity to give free vent to this predilection and the result was a superb interpretation.

*Appalachian Spring* won the New York Music Critics award and the Pulitzer prize in 1945. Copland asked Martha Graham to go with him to Carnegie Hall to accept the New York Music Critics award. After the ceremony, because he realized how great her contribution had been, he said, "You should have been up there with me, Martha." With characteristic humility she told him, "But I didn't write the music, Aaron—you did."

APPALACHIAN SPRING
Copyright 1945 by Aaron Copland. Reprinted by permission of Aaron
Copland, copyright owner, and Boosey and Hawkes, Inc., sole pub-
lishers and licensees.

# 19

## *Cultural Ambassador*

With World War II in progress in Europe, the United States began to give more serious consideration to the problem of creating stronger cultural ties with other countries of the western hemisphere. The threat of involvement in the conflict was becoming more obvious every day. In 1941, barely five months before the country actually went to war, Copland was chosen by Nelson Rockefeller, then Coordinator for Inter-American Affairs, to visit several countries of Latin America on what he called a "cultural mission."

It would have been difficult to find an important American artist more suited for this assignment. Copland's inherent sense of diplomacy and his almost European manners and courtesy were valuable assets in the new role. This was to be a four-month goodwill tour, ex-

tending from August to December, and Copland's responsibilities were to include lecturing, arranging concerts,
and conducting.

Supplied with scores by many contemporary American
composers, Aaron's first stop was Mexico. Here he was
familiar with the country and well known to many people; it was only on the next stop, in Colombia, that he
began to feel the immensity of the South American continent and the rich diversity of its many cultures.

After Colombia, he visited Ecuador, then Peru, Chile,
Uruguay, and Argentina. His time in the vast country of
Brazil, on the homeward journey, was a highly stimulating stop on his tour. It was, Copland thought, one of the
most progressive and promising of the countries he had
visited.

In Brazil the fusion of racial and cultural elements was
so complete that already an indigenous style in many of
the arts was emerging—unlike most of Latin America
where European influence was so strong that it hindered
the development of original art forms.

Copland saw and heard evidence of this native musical
life, particularly in the northern coastal towns of Brazil—
Recife, Baía, and Fortaleza. In Recife, he was honored
by a concert devoted to a demonstration of the local popular arts. One dance in particular had "terrific bounce."
It was the *frevo,* a solo dance whose accompanying music
is derived from street marches in much the same way that
jazz developed from the music played in New Orleans
funeral processions and other parades.

Each new town opened up a new musical experience

and in Baía, Copland heard for the first time an instrument called the *berimbau,* probably of Moorish origin. After the sophisticated concert life of Rio de Janeiro, São Paulo, and Buenos Aires, this lusty, throbbing music was a welcome change.

In spite of the whirlwind of traveling, with all the new experiences and distractions, Copland was able to continue work on a composition he had brought along with him. The Piano Sonata, dedicated to the American playwright Clifford Odets, who had commissioned it, was first performed in Buenos Aires. At first the work seemed difficult and "unyielding" to many who heard it. There is a curious wistfulness about the music and also the quality of timelessness that pervades so much of Copland's work. Wilfred Mellers, in a burst of poetic criticism, wrote of the ". . . andante which is a quintessential expression of immobility.The tender, cool melody, with its widely spaced fifths and fourths, floats out of the material of the scherzo and trio and comes to rest in empty harmonies that pulse as unobtrusively as a heartbeat." At the end ". . . the music runs down like a clock, dissolving away into space and eternity."

Copland suggested that it would be a good plan to establish several music centers in South America which would be supplied with the principal published works of North American composers. There was a great need of scores, orchestral parts, and chamber music works, as well as pamphlets with explanatory notes about the composers and their work.

South America evidently provided Copland with a

propitious atmosphere for work because on his second trip there in 1947—again as a goodwill ambassador for the State Department—he was able to finish the Clarinet Concerto which he wrote especially for the distinguished American jazz musician, Benny Goodman.

During the middle nineteen-forties, Copland's almost incessant traveling continued. During this period he was composing one of his major works—the Third Symphony. For a time he worked in Bernardsville, New Jersey; then he returned to New York City, after which he moved on to Ridgefield, Connecticut. His responsibilities at Tanglewood kept him busy until August when he made yet another move to the MacDowell Colony in New Hampshire. There, during the last months of summer in a remodeled stable, he finally finished the symphony. There was barely time for the necessary copying of the parts for the first performance with Koussevitzky and the Boston Symphony on October 18, 1946.

With the Third Symphony Copland hit his stride in big forms. The work is large in design and richly imaginative in details which are ingeniously worked into the entire pattern. There are four movements, the first of which is broad and expressive. At once it evokes the general character of the entire work, almost a "glorified and expansive hymn—of prayer, of praise, of sorrow, of patriotic sentiment." The second movement is a sprightly scherzo, the third is the adantino, and the fourth, a massive restatement of the opening themes with which the work began.

Almost as though Copland was calmly reflecting upon past experiences, there are remote suggestions of a leisurely, carefree cowboy tune, and then, as his reverie changed direction, a swift unleashing of Latin-American rhythm.

The critics were full of the warmest praise. Some spoke of the "brilliant orchestration . . . the abundance of harmonic and rhythmic invention." Others wrote of the work as being "broadly conceived and masterfully executed . . . almost a liberation . . . his freest outburst to date and paradoxically his most disciplined."

In 1944 Copland lectured at Harvard. (He had first been there in 1935 when he substituted for Walter Piston.) Now he was appointed to the Horatio Appleton Lamb chair, as later, in 1951–52, he would be appointed to the Charles Eliot Norton chair of poetry, the first American composer to be so honored. The Norton lectureship is a distinguished and important position; Copland felt that it was one of the greatest honors which he had yet received.

During this year Copland lived at the home of Mr. and Mrs. Edward Forbes. Forbes was a grandson of the American writer and poet, Ralph Waldo Emerson. It was an appropriate residence for Copland's year at Harvard, and while he was there he felt that he came much closer to an understanding of the New England spirit. He enormously enjoyed this period of his life, partly because he had never been a university student and he was now in daily contact with the academic life that he had missed.

That it was highly stimulating and thought-provoking is evidenced in his book *Music and Imagination,* developed from the Norton lectures. Perhaps part of its success can be attributed to the year of contact with so many thoughtful, talented young people. But whether he was working directly with them or not, Copland has always been keenly aware of the importance of education in the arts, and of inculcating a deep understanding of what creativity means to the life of an individual and to the nation.

Summing up these thoughts he said in one lecture:

Creativity in our country depends largely on fostering and understanding the role of the creative artist; he and his work must be made meaningful to each community. When creativity is understood as the activity of free and independent men, intent upon the reflection and summation of our own time in beautiful works, art in America will have entered on its most important phase.

# 20

# *Ding Dong House and the Villa Aurelia*

After so many years of constant traveling, Copland felt the need of a permanent home. New York City could no longer offer him the quiet or peace that he required; only more of the same frenetic pace that he had to cope with on his travels. It had become increasingly difficult as a place to live. By the late nineteen-forties its air had become foul, traffic was maddening, and rents were climbing beyond reach. The time had come to make a move outside the city. Copland chose a quiet village known as Sneden's Landing, about three quarters of an hour from New York, long a favorite of writers and theater people. The house was called, for some unknown reason, Ding Dong House. It proved to be the perfect setting in which to write a work that has come to be con-

174

sidered one of Copland's finest achievements—the Emily Dickinson song cycle.

Part of the rambling white colonial structure had been built in prerevolutionary times. Outside were wide lawns and old trees, a trellis over the front porch was covered in summer with the bright leaves of a grapevine. In the autumn, large clumps of dark Concord grapes hung down, tempting visitors who rapidly lost interest when they tasted the sour fruit.

To one side of the house was a secluded yard with peony beds and old lilac bushes where one could almost see a ghostly Emily wandering in the shadows as she wrote her letter to the world. The lawn to the rear of the house, once set in formal gardens, sloped down to the Hudson River where the nights were made more beautiful by the flashing lights of Tarrytown on the opposite bank.

Through the summer and winter of 1950, Aaron wandered about the house with a book of Emily's poems almost always in his hand. The more he read, the more intrigued he became with the stark New England simplicity of her style.

Copland had been casting around for quite a while for some American poetry that he could set to music. He had often considered the work of Walt Whitman, especially one poem called "Come, Heavenly Death," which had fascinated him for a long time. But as much as he wanted to use Whitman's poetry, he always came to the same conclusion: there was a strong "prose rhythm" about the work that was too powerful to set to music.

Then, one day when he was searching through an

anthology of poetry, his eye caught Emily Dickinson's poem which begins "Because I could not stop for Death. . . ." It had the brooding, mysterious quality that is typical of the poet's best work—a haunting mood that had a strong appeal for Aaron. He set to work immediately.

> Because I could not stop for Death,
> He kindly stopped for me;
> The carriage held but just ourselves
> And Immortality.
>
> We slowly drove, he knew no haste,
> And I had put away
> My labor, and my leisure too,
> For his civility.
>
> We passed the school where children played,
> Their lessons scarcely done;
> We passed the fields of gazing grain,
> We passed the setting sun.
>
> We paused before a house that seemed
> A swelling of the ground;
> The roof was scarcely visible,
> The cornice but a mound.
>
> Since then 'tis centuries; but each
> Feels shorter than the day
> I first surmised the horses' heads
> Were toward eternity.

Within two weeks Aaron had completed the song. His intention had been to write only one song but in the two

# 12. The Chariot

Music by
AARON COPLAND

THE CHARIOT
From Twelve Poems of Emily Dickinson. Music by Aaron Copland.
Copyright 1951 by Aaron Copland, copyright owner, and Boosey
and Hawkes, Inc., sole publishers and licensees. (Text of poem is as
it appears in song.)

weeks of actual work, his already considerable interest in Emily Dickinson's poetry had become passionate. He read all her poems and began on the biographies of her life. He decided to write two more songs, and three months later he felt impelled to write still another three. Eventually he wrote twelve songs to Emily Dickinson's poems—a complete song cycle that had as its concluding poem the one that he had begun with.

Each of the major categories into which the poems fall is represented: nature, life, love, time, and eternity. Copland's music masterfully evokes the poet's austere and brooding world. Hearing the music helps one to visualize that world more intensely as it conjures up the late afternoon shadows on a white clapboard house, a rustle of lilac leaves in the evening wind, or a lonely figure brooding on the nature of death.

Again, the enigma of Copland's art raises the familiar questions. Why is it that a musician of so urban a background, of such a highly sophisticated musical sense is able to convey with such mastery the remote quality of pastoral America in the nineteenth century?

Many answers have been given, among which Copland's must surely carry the most weight: that which we attempt to describe in literary terms and associate with a particular time or place is in reality the abstract, intangible—and indescribable inner quality of one individual.

In 1946, Aaron met the young man who was to become, in the early nineteen-fifties, the librettist for his opera *The Tender Land*. Erik Johns (who wrote under the pseudonym of Horace Everett) was one of those unusually versatile young artists who seem to appear at certain intervals in the history of art. He was an accomplished dancer, painter, and writer; in fact, in the arts he was a jack-of-all-trades and master of several.

Erik became a frequent visitor to Ding Dong House, bringing with him many other young people who were working in other art fields. Their spirited enthusiasms were a great delight to Aaron, who has always been especially interested in helping young artists. There were painters, writers, and designers, although musicians were still the most frequent guests. Jerome Robbins, the choreographer who later had great success in shows such as *West Side Story*, came frequently. Agnes de Mille, the choreographer, was another visitor to Ding Dong House. And always among the most welcome of guests was Minna Lederman, a fond old friend and editor of *Modern Music*.

Several of Erik Johns's stories had a strong theatrical quality that interested Copland. One day as they discussed certain problems of character development and story construction, it became clear to Aaron that he had found the librettist he had been seeking for several years.

Stored in his files was a considerable amount of music he had written for an intended Broadway production based on *Tragic Ground*, a book by Erskine Caldwell. The project had strong appeal for Copland and he deeply regretted that the show, for a variety of reasons, was never put into production.

When Aaron and Erik discovered *Let Us Now Praise Famous Men,* by James Agee, they felt they had come upon fresh material which would be suitable for some of the music Aaron had written. Agee's book is a moving collection of essays that describe the lives of the desperately poor tenant farmers of the South. During the bitter years of the depression, few groups of people suffered greater hardships than the rural poor, hardships which made the photographs illustrating the book unforgettable. These were the work of the talented young photographer Walker Evans, who accompanied Agee on his trip through the South.

Copland played some of the music for Erik and discussed the possibility of collaborating on a new theatrical work which would be based upon *Let Us Now Praise Famous Men* but use the music written for *Tragic Ground.* Erik spent several days poring over the photographs and found himself returning again and again to one of a mother and a young girl who had been hardened by the deprivations of the time but still seemed to possess vigor and hope for the future. He began to surmise what might happen if this girl were to break the pattern of her mother's life, to cut herself off from the rural tradition that had been such an important part of her family's history.

After working together for several months, both Johns and Copland realized that their joint efforts had led them to an entirely new concept. Because the work began to have an operatic quality that would not do for Broadway, they decided to abandon all the earlier material for *Let Us Now Praise Famous Men.*

The final version of this work, which was eventually titled *The Tender Land,* was commissioned by Richard Rodgers and Oscar Hammerstein II for the thirtieth anniversary of the League of Composers and was performed by the New York City Opera Company under the direction of Thomas Schippers.

The opening bars sound the soft, widely spaced chords that have come to be known as typical of Copland's work. He evokes the mood and atmosphere of the scene with the easy mastery of the creator confident of his powers. Slowly the curtain rises on the setting of a fertile Middle Western landscape, its white clapboard farmhouse painted in the spirit of Grant Wood's pristine American landscapes. It is here, within a dawn-to-dusk time span that all the action takes place. The leading characters are the Moss family, Ma, her two daughters Laurie and Beth, and their grandfather. Martin and Top are two drifters who provoke the grandfather's suspicion, and when Laurie falls in love with Martin, the conflict begins.

Laurie is about to graduate from high school, and her future seems to rest on the decision that she must now make. As she weighs her love for her family and the local traditions against the fascination of Martin and an exciting future far from home, the opera reaches a moving and poignant climax.

Strong dramatic action on the stage is limited but there is much musical variety that makes up for it. There are some fine ensembles, such as the quintet called "The Promise of Living" and a very beautiful love duet sung by Laurie and Martin. The dissonances are subtle—as before the final cadence—and seem to suggest the under-

THE TENDER LAND
Copyright 1956 by Aaron Copland. Reprinted by permission of Aaron
Copland, copyright owner, and Boosey and Hawkes, Inc., sole pub-
lishers and licensees.

current of doubt and uncertainty about the young girl's
future. Throughout, the score is characterized by a quality of clean, pure sound that seems exactly right for the
subject of the opera.

*The Tender Land* received a tremendous ovation from
the first-night audience but, as Copland said later, "the
house must have been full of friends." The reviews were
not favorable and were particularly critical of the libretto.
They called it sentimental and without sufficient depth.
The characters remained two-dimensional, familiar pro-
totypes of the period. Both Copland and Johns felt the

criticisms were well taken and set to work on the re-
visions. After much work, the final version was shortened
to one hour and forty minutes. *The Tender Land* became
a great favorite as a vehicle for high school workshops
and is widely performed throughout the country.

In the early nineteen-fifties, Copland received another
opportunity to live abroad for an extended period of time.
He had never visited Rome for more than a few weeks
but it had been long enough for him to feel what has been
called "the fatal charm of Italy." Now, returning as a
visiting artist to the American Academy, he would be
able to enjoy the many pleasures of Rome with only the
minimum discomforts that are so well known to anyone
who has ever wintered in the Eternal City.

The American Academy, which was once the Villa
Aurelia, is situated on the Janiculum, one of the famous
seven hills of ancient Rome. It is near the outskirts of the
city and just within the famous Aurelian wall, which
takes its name from the Emperor Marcus Aurelius.

Since 1894, the year of its establishment, young artists
have competed for the privileges of residence at the
Academy. To stimulate these young people, and oc-
casionally offer a critical eye or ear, mature artists are
generally invited to spend the better part of a year at the
Academy. When Aaron Copland was given an invitation,
he decided to share his good fortune with two friends,
Erik Johns and the talented young choreographer Louisa
Krebs. He arranged for them to have studios in the Via
Margutta, one of the old artist sections of Rome.

The city is a distracting place for the visiting artist.

The Romans' love of elegant display, the endless fascinations of the old city, the problems of adequate heat and hot water in the winter are only some of the problems that beset him. Perhaps most dangerous of all is the sense of history, the "weight" of history that many artists have found so overpowering they have been unable to accomplish anything at all.

Most of the week was spent in work but on at least two afternoons Aaron would meet Erik and Louisa to show them the different parts of the city that he knew and loved.

They would generally meet at Erik's studio and then walk down the famous Via Margutta, past its old studios and courtyards in the direction of the Piazza di Spagna. The beautiful Piazza and its famous steps have been a meeting place for foreigners and artists for centuries. At one time the steps were crowded with costumed models who came there to be hired by the artists of the neighborhood.

Aaron pointed out No. 5 on the Piazza, where Mendelssohn had lived. Along with so many other foreign musicians who had visited the city, he had been appalled at the quality of its musical performances and had written that "it is so wretched that it is really beneath all criticism."

Although Aaron showed his friends most of the historical sights and museums, they still found time to study what is perhaps one of the greatest attractions of Rome —life in the streets.

A particularly favorite way of ending the afternoon

would be a stroll through the gardens of the Pincio, where at sunset there are superb views of the city with its hundreds of church domes and the silver strip of the Tiber in the distance. On the way back to the Via Marguttta they would pass the Villa Medici, which is now the French Academy, the place where the twenty-year-old Debussy had been so homesick and miserable. Copland could never pass the place without thinking of the composer whose show music had been one of the greatest joys of his early years.

Poor Debussy had called the Villa Medici (which had been designed with the assistance of Michelangelo for the Medici Pope Leo X) "the abominable villa" and found the whole of Rome "positively ugly—a town of marble, fleas, and boredom."

Toward the end of his stay, Aaron was able fully to understand the legendary charm of Rome, so powerful that it had completely overwhelmed many visiting artists who decided never to return home. He enjoyed his stay there and took pleasure in working with the young musicians at the Academy. Nevertheless, it was with a growing impatience that he made plans to leave Europe and return to his new home near New York.

# 2 1

# Aaron Copland—
# Dean of American
# Composers

Aaron Copland has long been one of the most financially successful composers in the world. And financial security has seldom been a familiar state for the composer of serious music. As late as the nineteen-sixties it was estimated that only five or six composers were able to make a satisfactory living from their music alone.

It is unfortunate that this struggle is such an old one. Even Mozart and Beethoven had to earn their living in part as pianists, and Mozart's money troubles were never resolved in the course of his short life. Schubert almost starved to death. And Gustav Mahler lived in fear that his brief months of "vacation"—as director of the Vienna Opera and the Philharmonic—would not be sufficient for the composition of his own work.

186

Even when a score is published in printed form and widely performed, royalties are not considerable. A dozen performances of a symphony may bring in as little as three hundred dollars to the composer and an equal amount to the publisher. The only substantial profits are to be made from theater and film music, the two fields from which Copland has received a handsome return. And yet even here, when these works are recorded, half goes to the publisher.

Another source of income has been Copland's books, which have gone into dozens of printings and been widely translated. He is a fluent writer and has been able to put complex musical ideas in a form that has had great appeal for the general public. His first book, *What to Listen For in Music,* published in 1939, was composed of the first fifteen lectures he gave at the New School for Social Research. It had never occurred to Copland to publish the talks until an editor of the McGraw-Hill Book Company, who had been an interested auditor, came up one night after the talk was over and suggested the idea to him.

*What to Listen For in Music* is a valuable guide to a better understanding of the creative process and the elements of "musical anatomy"—rhythm, melody, and simple harmonic structure. Deems Taylor called it the best book of its kind he had ever seen. Twenty years after its original publication, Copland added some new chapters on contemporary music, a new discography of long-playing records and the book again became a best seller—in its field—in the paperback market.

*Our New Music,* Copland's second book, follows the development of contemporary music in America and Europe and contains excerpts from some of his critical reviews that had been published in *Modern Music,* the *New Republic,* and the *American Mercury.*

His third book, *Music and Imagination,* is another work which came out of a lecture series, in this case, the six talks Copland gave when he held the Charles Eliot Norton chair of poetry at Harvard during the 1951–52 academic year. In the preface he wrote:

> . . . the six talks were not intended to be closely reasoned arguments on a single subject, but rather a free improvisation on the general theme of the role imagination plays in the art of music. The first half of the book treats of the musical mind at work in its different capacities as listener, interpreter or creator. The second half discusses more specifically recent manifestations of the imaginative mind in the music of Europe and the Americas.

*Copland on Music,* published in 1960, is a collection of several articles, talks, and excerpts from his journal and reviews. It contains an interesting survey of personalities in the world of music and is a more informal exposition of his ideas than the previous books.

Copland is an articulate writer whose deep insight into the nature of music has often inspired him to analyze the psychology of music. In an extremely interesting passage, for example, he describes and comments on an audience's fascination with the *flow* of music, and its alarm

when that music is interrupted before it has been allowed
to come to a natural conclusion. He has also been interested in the general form a musician's life may take, in
his economic problems, and in the effects that his music
has on his listeners. It is because of this wide-ranging interest in music as a *phenomenon* that Copland's writing
has gone beyond that of many other composers whose
literary efforts are often rather vaguely worded comments
on the intangible nature and fascination of music. Aaron
Copland has shown an unusual ability to give his ideas
substantial literary form.

Copland tried to buy Ding Dong House but its owners
refused to sell. After much searching, and a few false
moves, he finally purchased a secluded contemporary
house not far from Peekskill, New York. Situated on a
promontory that rises from thickly wooded terrain, the
house commands a beautiful view of the distant Hudson
River to the west. The house is very simply furnished;
there is the feeling, as in his music, that nothing here is
extraneous. Every object must have a function or be discarded. His spacious studio, with walls of glass on two
sides, is furnished with a few chairs, a large, plain table
that serves as a desk, many books, and, of course, a grand
piano. Rock Hill, as the estate is called, offers Copland
the seclusion and quiet that he needs, particularly after
one of his frequent journeys in the United States or
abroad. Almost everywhere he goes he is asked to conduct but there are frequent lectures and appearances on
television as well. A major effort in this field was his nar-

ration for a series of television programs by the National Education Network that vividly brought to life the musical developments of the nineteen-twenties.

During the past few years Copland has realized more than ever how important it is for the composer-conductor of today to be multilingual. The international language of musical terms is only the first section of the bridge that a conductor must cross if he is to communicate fully with a foreign orchestra.

Time for rehearsals is usually limited; furthermore, even the best translators are of little use in helping a player understand delicate shades and nuances of feeling. The German-speaking countries present few problems because Copland has a firm grasp of the language, the result of his many visits to Germany and Austria, together with a good deal of solitary study. But the Poles, who are not sufficiently proficient in French, are still hostile to the use of German, and Copland cannot accommodate them in Polish. Linguistically, Copland is probably as much at home in French as he is in English. His Spanish is "adequate." And yet problems still arise, as in Japan where he had to work exclusively through an interpreter. "It wasn't much fun at all," he confided later to a friend.

With the call to conduct and speak in many foreign lands came honors, degrees, and awards. He has received honorary degrees from many outstanding universities, including Princeton and Harvard.

In 1961 the first of several invitations to the White House came. On the first occasion Pablo Casals was the guest soloist at one of the most elegant and distinguished musical soirees the White House had ever given. Besides many well-known patrons of music there were several conductors, including Leopold Stokowski and Eugene Ormandy. Among the many other distinguished composers there were Samuel Barber and Leonard Bernstein. "Why," Copland told a friend on his return, "there must have been twenty composers there!"

President John F. Kennedy, who had focused government attention on the arts for the first time in the history of the country, spoke on the state of the arts. He talked of the need to regard music as an integral part of a free society. "The work of all artists, musicians, painters, designers, and architects," he said, "stands as a symbol of human freedom."

It was the beginning, Copland hoped, of the much longed-for government subsidy of the arts—a cause which has always been of the utmost importance to him.

Copland has been especially interested in the overall cultural climate of the country. Answering people who believe that creativity is the same everywhere in the world, he said: "My observation and experience convince me of two things: first, that the notion of the creative man plays a less important role here than is true in other countries, and second, that it is especially necessary that we, the artists of America, make clear to our countrymen the value attached in all lands to the idea of the creative personality."

In Europe, the patronage of the nobility had long centuries ago planted among the common people a seed of respect and even of awe toward the arts. Withstanding centuries of change, that attitude has persisted until the present day when art is now within the reach of everyone.

America, with its heritage of the common man struggling for his very livelihood in an uncivilized continent, has fostered a different attitude toward art, which is still basically regarded as an adornment rather than an integral and essential part of life. As a consequence, artists —except for the relatively few who have achieved reputations—are still without real prestige or status within the American civilization.

Aaron Copland knew that government subsidies would do much to help raise that status in the eyes of all citizens. Writing in *Copland on Music,* he said: "People often tend to reflect attitudes of constituted authority. Our people will show more concern for their artists as soon as the government shows more concern for the welfare of art in America." Although government support has increased in recent years, he believes that it is still a bare trickle compared to what is needed if the arts in America are to flourish.

Copland also regrets the fact that much of what passes as culture today is an obsession with the *idea* of culture rather than a true and meaningful experience of art. There is an unholy emphasis on size and volume—great new museums, an incessant flow of sound—without any genuinely deep involvement in art itself.

Once at a party a rather insensitive man who wished to ingratiate himself with Copland said that the first thing he did on a Saturday morning was to pile the phonograph with long-playing records and keep it going throughout the day as he attended to his work about the house. Copland said nothing but was horrified to realize how little music really meant to such a man.

Later he wrote:

Music has become so very accessible it is almost impossible to avoid it. Perhaps you don't mind cashing a check at the local bank to the strains of a Brahms symphony but I do. Actually, I think I spend as much time avoiding great works as others spend in seeking them out. The reason is simple; meaningful music demands one's undivided attention, and I can give it that only when I am in a receptive mood, and feel the need for it. The use of music as a kind of ambrosia to titillate the aural sense while one's conscious mind is otherwise occupied is the abomination of every composer who takes his work seriously.

On Aaron Copland's sixty-fifth birthday, congratulations and words of praise arrived from all over the world. It has become an expected commonplace for admirers of famous men to praise their personal and human attributes as well as their mastery of their particular art. This was true of many of the messages which Copland received, but there was also an unusual ring of deep sincerity underlining the usual sentiments.

Minna Lederman, his old friend, wrote: "The good fortune of co-existence gives us a special share in his excellence—in the nature, the light, and the power that have shaped our time."

Jerome Robbins, the choreographer, wrote: "Happy

Birthday, dear Aaron—and thank you for the inspiration and illumination you have given to all who have performed, conducted, sung, danced to, worked with, or just listened to your music. The music is like you, Aaron; it is tender, clear, powerful, intelligent, witty, accurate, and sensitive. It is suffused with love, strong in structure. We thank you for it and for you."

Elie Siegmeister, the composer, wrote: ". . . you blazed many bright and savage paths for American music, showed that New York need not always be a suburb of Paris or Vienna, tempered Walt Whitman's 'wild, barbaric yawp' with fine sensibility and elegant know-how."

One of the strongest characteristics of Aaron Copland's work is a feeling of open space, the evocation of a simpler pastoral life. Critics often comment on these qualities and hear in his music the powerful expression of this great natural beauty; they speak too of the serenity and sense of tranquillity that one associates with our vast windswept prairies.

More thoughtful critics understood that Copland's music is not an expression of the great prairies as much as it is the *urban longing* for the pastoral life of a different period.

In an old Appalachian folk song called "Nottamin Town" the singer tells of his experience in the big city, "Ten thousand around me and I was alone." Copland's music tells of this loneliness too.

And yet it is curious that this composer's work strikes such a deep chord of longing and nostalgia for the peace and gentleness of nature. Copland as a man was never drawn to the land. Unlike so many other creative people, he never dreamed of actually participating in country life. He is the last man on earth one expects to see out on the threshing field or coming into the house with pails of milk, the smell of the barn still about him.

It is an enigma and a paradox that this musician who is among the most urbane of artists should voice so powerfully these longings within each of us. Copland himself suggests that this quality in his music is an expression of his own inner calm, a tranquillity which in the minds of most listeners is associated with nature.

Perhaps Copland's music speaks also of the longing for the open country felt by a people who were for centuries forbidden by law from ownership of land. It is this single fact which is responsible for much of the character which Jewish culture was to take during the long centuries of seclusion. Aaron Copland's ancestors, the Jews of Russia, were not only confined to villages and small cities but were barred from Moscow and St. Petersburg. Only privileged individuals with special permits were allowed to live there.

That the wandering Jew was an exile, all the world knew. But that he also shared in the common human longing to work the land, to sing of its harsh demands, and wondrous rewards has not frequently been commented on during the long centuries of his oppression.

When one realizes that the Yiddish of the eastern European Jews contains the names of only two flowers (the rose and the violet) and none of the names of wild birds, the realization of what "the ghetto" really meant strikes home with renewed force.

Yet another explanation for these qualities in Copland's music might be his father's intense love and admiration for America. Some of his earliest memories from childhood recall his father's great pride in being an American and of the great privilege it is to be an American.

Aaron Copland has not followed the religion of his parents. He is an agnostic but one who is deeply aware of the grandeur and mystery of the universe. When speaking of religion, Copland refers to the vastness of space and "the sense of oneself in the universe."

"And isn't that religion," he asks, ". . . that connection with something larger than oneself?" Perhaps it is another statement of the belief that the ultimate purpose of religion is union with that state or being for which men have found so many different names. For Aaron Copland that way has always been music.

# Musical Works
# by Aaron Copland

OPERA
>   The Second Hurricane [1937]
>   The Tender Land [1954]

BALLETS
>   Appalachian Spring [1944]
>   Ballet (Untitled) [1959]
>   Billy The Kid [1938]
>   Grogh [1925]
>   Hear Ye! Hear Ye! [1934]
>   Rodeo [1942]

FILM SCORES
>   The City [1939]
>   The Cummington Story [1945]
>   The Heiress [1949]
>   North Star [1943]
>   Of Mice and Men [1939]

*Our Town* [*1940*]
*The Red Pony* [*1948*]

INCIDENTAL MUSIC
FOR STAGE AND TELEVISION
*The Five Kings* [*1939*]
*From Sorcery to Science* [*1939*]
*Miracle at Verdun* [*1931*]
*Quiet City* [*1940*]
*The World of Nick Adams* [*1957*]

ORCHESTRAL WORKS
*Appalachian Spring. Suite from the ballet* [*1944*]
*Billy the Kid: Suite from the ballet* [*1938*]
*Billy the Kid: Suite from the ballet: Nos. 3 and 5* [*1938*]
*Billy the Kid: Waltz from the ballet* [*1938*]
*Concerto for Piano and Orchestra* [*1926*]
*Cortège Macabre* [*1923*]
*Dance Symphony* [*1925*]
*Danzón Cubano* [*1942–1944*]
*Fanfare for the Common Man* [*1942*]
*Fantasia Mexicana* [*1936*]
*First Symphony* [*1928*]
*John Henry* [*1940 revised 1952*]
*Jubilee Variation* [*1945*]
*Letter from Home* [*1944; revised 1962*]
*Lincoln Portrait* [*1942*]
*Music for a Great City* [*1964*]
*Music for Radio* [*1937*]
*Music for the Movies* [*1942*]
*Music for the Theatre* [*1925*]
*Orchestral Variations* [*1957*]
*Our Town. Music from the Film* [*1940*]
*An Outdoor Overture* [*1938*]
*Preamble for a Solemn Occasion* [*1949*]

*Quiet City [1940]*
*The Red Pony. Suite from the film [1948]*
*Rodeo: Four Dance Episodes from the ballet [1942]*
*El Salón México [1936]*
*Short Symphony (No. 2) [1933]*
*Statements [1934]*
*Symphonic Ode [1929 revised 1955]*
*Symphony for Organ and Orchestra [1924]*
*Third Symphony [1946]*
*The Tender Land: Orchestral Suite [1957]*
*Two Mexican Pieces [1959]*

WORKS FOR STRING ORCHESTRA
*Concerto for Clarinet and String Orchestra with Harp and*
*Piano [1948]*
*Rodeo: Hoe-Down [1942]*
*Two Pieces [1928]*

WORKS FOR BAND
*Billy the Kid. Suite from the ballet: Nos. 5 & 8 [1938]*
*Emblems for Symphonic Band [1964]*
*Lincoln Portrait [1942]*
*An Outdoor Overture [1938]*
*Variations on a Shaker Melody [1956]*

CHAMBER MUSIC
*As It Fell Upon A Day [1923]*
*Elegies [1932]*
*Nonet [1960]*
*Quartet for Piano and Strings [1950]*
*Sextet [1937]*
*Two Pieces for String Quartet [1928]*
*Vitebsk [1929]*

VIOLIN AND PIANO
*Billy the Kid: Suite from the ballet: Nos. 5 & 8 [1938]*
*Rodeo: Hoe-Down [1942]*

*Sonata for Violin and Piano* [*1943*]
*Two Pieces* [*1926*]

VIOLONCELLO AND PIANO
*Billy the Kid: Suite from the ballet: Nos. 5 & 8* [*1938*]
*Billy the Kid: Waltz from the ballet* [*1938*]

CLARINET & PIANO
*Concerto for Clarinet* [*1948*]

PIANO SOLO
*Billy the Kid: Suite from the ballet: Nos. 1, 2, 5 & 8*
  [*1938*]
*Billy the Kid: Waltz from the ballet* [*1938*]
*The Cat and the Mouse* [*1920*]
*Dance Panels* [*1959; revised 1962*]
*Danzón Cubano* [*1942–1945*]
*Down a Country Lane* [*1962*]
*El Salón México* [*1936*]
*Four Piano Blues* [*1948*]
*Fantasia Mexicana* [*1936*]
*Our Town* [*1940*]
*Passacaglia* [*1922*]
*Piano Fantasy* [*1957*]
*Piano Variations* [*1930*]
*Sentimental Melody* [*1926*]
*Sonata for Piano* [*1941*]
*Two Children's Pieces* [*1936*]

TWO PIANOS
*Billy the Kid: Suite from the ballet: Nos. 1, 2 & 5 to 8*
  [*1938*]
*Billy the Kid: Waltz from the ballet* [*1938*]
*Concerto for Piano* [*1926*]
*Danzón Cubano* [*1942–1945*]
*El Salón Mexico* [*1936*]
*Rodeo: Dance Episodes Nos. 3 & 4* [*1942*]

ORGAN SOLO
> *Episode [1941]*
> *Preamble for a Solemn Occasion [1949]*
> *Symphony for Organ and Orchestra [1924]*

VOCAL MUSIC
> *Dirge in Woods [1954]*
> *Old American Songs. Set I [1950]*
> *Old American Songs. Set II [1952]*
> *Old Poem [1920]*
> *Pastorale [1921]*
> *Song [1927]*
> *The Tender Land: Laurie's Song [1954]*
> *Twelve Poems of Emily Dickinson [1950]*
> *Vocalise [1928]*

CHORAL MUSIC
> *Las Agachadas: 'The Shake-down Song' [1942]*
> *Canticle of Freedom [1955; revised 1965]*
> *Four Motets [1921]*
> *In the Beginning [1947]*
> *Lark [1938]*
> *North Star (Two Choruses from the Film Music) [1943]*
> *Old American Songs. Set I [1950]*
> *Old American Songs. Set II, No. 5 [1952]*
> *The Tender Land: Choral Square Dance 'Stomp Your Foot' [1954]*
> *The Tender Land: 'The Promise of Living' (Thanksgiving Song) [1954]*
> *Two Choruses [1925]*
> *What Do We Plant? [1935]*

# Pocket Scores

SHORT SYMPHONY (*No. 2*)
STATEMENTS
SYMPHONIC ODE
SYMPHONY FOR ORGAN AND ORCHESTRA
SYMPHONY NO. 1
SYMPHONY NO. *3*
THE TENDER LAND *Suite from the opera*

# Scores For Young People

OPERA
*The Second Hurricane*

ORCHESTRAL WORKS
*Billy the Kid: Waltz from the ballet*
*Down a Country Lane*
*Letter from Home*
*An Outdoor Overture*
*Variations on a Shaker Melody (from Appalachian Spring)*

WORKS FOR BAND
*Billy the Kid. Suite from the ballet: Nos. 5 & 8*
*Lincoln Portrait*
*An Outdoor Overture*
*Variations on a Shaker Melody*

All inquiries concerning Aaron Copland's published scores should be directed to: Boosey and Hawkes, 30 West 57th Street, New York N.Y. 10019.

# Books by Aaron Copland

COPLAND ON MUSIC. New York: Doubleday and Company, Inc., 1960

MUSIC AND IMAGINATION. Cambridge, Massachusetts: Harvard University Press, 1961

OUR NEW MUSIC. New York: McGraw-Hill Book Company, Inc., 1941

WHAT TO LISTEN FOR IN MUSIC, rev. ed. New York: McGraw-Hill Book Company, 1957

# Index

206

## About the Author

As a long-time friend of Aaron Copland, Arnold Dobrin felt that he knew much about the composer's life that would interest young people. Although this is his first biographical work, Mr. Dobrin has written and illustrated several books for children.

A native of Omaha, Nebraska, Mr. Dobrin studied at the Chouinard Art Institute in Los Angeles, at the University of California at Los Angeles, and at the Academy de la Grande Chaumière in Paris. He lived in Rome for two years and has traveled extensively in Europe, Asia, and the Near East. Mr. Dobrin lives in Westport, Connecticut.